Letters from Malabar

And 'On the Way' – A Historical Glimpse of India at the Start of the 20th Century

By Henry Bruce

Published by Pantianos Classics

ISBN-13: 978-1-78987-091-6

First published in 1909

Contents

Introduction

I ACCEPTED Mr. Bruce's invitation to write a few words of introduction to this interesting volume, because I was fortunate enough to occupy for some time the post of British Resident in Travancore and Cochin, and have myself, in the pages of English reviews and elsewhere, attempted to describe the indescribable beauties of the Malabar coast and the fascination of life in the only part of the Indian

Here we see the conditions which prevailed before any invader violated the sacred soil of the Peninsula, and here linger the relations which existed in those days between the two sexes, and between the higher and the lower castes, and here we still see that faithful dispensation of the gifts of the gods, which entitles Travancore to claim to be in very truth the land of charity. Indeed the motto of the house of the able prince who rules over this, the larger of the two native principalities, is 'Charity our household divinity.'

Here you can live on the coast beside the sounding sea, and very loudly it does sound, in tracts of which the population is nearly 2000 to the square mile, or you can rise higher to 8000 feet, where often thick clouds settle down over grass and forests, and shroud the heights m impenetrable gloom, where you can bag the wild elephant, the rare and magnificent bison, the tiger, and other big game.

When the clouds lift, you can see revealed long, silent valleys, down which flow rivers to fertilise fields upon fields of rice before they are lost in the Arabian Sea.

In the forests you come upon big herds of elephants who live happily in the dense recesses of the dark wood, rendered negotiable only by paths they make for themselves, enjoying their favourite food, with a swamp on one side for a hath, and a grassy hill on the other for pasture.

Tree-trunks smothered in moss, and orchids, rhododendrons bearded with lichen, grassy glades, and many-coloured flowers, tree ferns, elephant reeds, cascades, and rivers, the sight of distant hills, and

> 'Valleys low where the mild whispers use
> Of shades and wanton winds and gushing brooks.'

Such are frequent phenomena of the march in this favoured land.

But if every prospect pleases, man, and no less women, are by no means vile. In the upper class women enjoy an independence unknown in any other

iv

part of the world, including the privilege of choosing and changing their own husbands, a privilege which they exercise with much discretion, rarely divorcing a husband if he turns out at all a possible person. Girls of the upper class, from fourteen to sixteen, are exceedingly beautiful. They possess perfect figures, lithe, slight, and supple, yet not wanting in development, and they wear costumes which modestly veil but heighten the charm of the wearer. Bright brown eyes, light brown skin, pearly teeth, and vivacious expression, go to make up a personality such as a classical painter, like Alma-Tadema, would love to paint, clad in flowing draperies, and moving over the tessellated pavement of pillared halls.

The Administration of this favoured land is as good as the country is beautiful, and, for my part, I greatly regret that ministers from without are inclined to regard reform as synonymous with destruction of individuality. The individuality of the states of Travancore and Cochin is a most precious possession, which, once lost, will never he replaced in any other part of the world, or in India itself. Nor is it apparent why people, who are happy and lightly taxed, should be reformed whether they will or not, while in many respects these two states are ahead of British India in civilisation.

Now that the railway has pierced these two principalities and scarred their sacred soil with iron hands, the traveller can, if he wishes, see for himself, and he will go away with a feeling that he has left behind him perhaps the most beautiful part of India.

J. D. Rees.

Author's Preface

First of all, I must express my thanks to the Editors of two of the leading Anglo-Indian journals. The whole of the following volume, with most of the illustrations here produced, and with others, appeared in the 'Times of India' a year or more ago. The three remaining articles, on the Administrations of the three Southern States, appeared in the 'Madras Mail' a little earlier.

At the opposite Northern and Southern ends of the Indian Empire lie the two rarest portions thereof, certainly the two Native States most uniquely favoured by Nature. Kashmir and Travancore are some 2000 miles apart as the crow would fly, essentially 3000 miles as one has to travel. It would take a week to get from one to the other, with the best aid of the slow Indian railways. It would be too much to say that their climates are the best and the worst in India. Kashmir has a quasi-European climate, deceptive (like its people), and apt to turn out much less healthy than you thought that it was at the beginning. My entire stay in Malabar was but four or five weeks, or about as many weeks as I have lived for years in Kashmir.

The climate of Malabar, at least in its southern parts, is one trying for the strongest European adults, and impossible for European children. This difference in climate may well explain the fact that, while a traveller seldom appears in Travancore, Kashmir is thronged with visitors – about two thousand of them per year. But it will not wholly explain the difference in the popular renown of the two countries. Even in the world of the Arabian Nights, and in the earlier Chinese world, Kashmir had a great fame. As a result of this fact, and of its many visitors throughout the centuries, the books about Kashmir, often excellent and richly illustrated, are innumerable.

I have already publicly presented the case for the restoration of his remaining powers to the kindly Maharaja of Kashmir, who is, of course, no Kashmiri, but the grandson of one of the more considerable conquerors of the nineteenth century. He ascended the throne in the same year with the Maharaja of Travancore, 1885. The area of his dominions is about that of Great Britain. It may here be said that, by the latest accounts, Kashmir, which was for so long the Paradise of the adventurous traveller, but which has long been spoiling, is now utterly spoiled, to the point that English ladies can hardly venture abroad there with safety. Travellers may well begin to turn their attention elsewhere.

Malabar is the magical coast-land which has been defined as extending from Canara to Cape Comorin. This, too, has always had a peculiar, although a less noisy, fame. Rousseau, in a little-known passage summing up the picturesque impressions of India which had reached the Europe of his day, speaks of *'les Malabars. le Mogul, les rives du Gange.'* Some of the echoes of its fame have been due to its peculiar customs, rightly or wrongly understood. In an appendix to one of the earlier volumes of his great 'History of France,' now seventy-five years old, Michelet casually refers to Malabar as *'le pays le plus corrompu de l'Inde.'* When I quoted this passage to Mr. Rees, he wrote back: 'I don't agree with Michelet.' Ethnologists and others interested in the subject, are aware that Malabar actually offers some physiological peculiarities in c the female form divine,' which has always flourished there. A universally learned German once made the Rabelaisian remark: 'By all means go to Malabar; they have excellent dairies there.' A knowledge of German will increase the appreciation of this saying.

Malabar certainly offers a social peculiarity which is passing strange, and fascinating as being found nowhere else upon this broad earth, unless among some South Sea savages or the like. It is a cynical saying, even in Europe: 'It is a wise child who knows his own father.' In Malabar it is unnecessary, or at least unimportant, to know your father: it is your mother who counts, for all purposes of inheritance. How beautifully this system of matriarchy solves certain problems! Was this the primeval system throughout the world, before the patriarchal system arose, to decline in its turn? In that ease Malabar is, indeed, a priceless survival from the earlier ages. Or have its people invented or developed matriarchy on their own? I leave it wholly to the learned to answer these questions. In any event, the situation is consummately interesting.

I do not write for those who cannot feel the appeal of the vastness and the variety of India. Travancore is, roughly, but one-250th part, in mere area, of that wonderful Empire. In population, it is about one-100th part of India. But in true interest, importance, and, above all, uniqueness, it is enormously more than either of the above proportions would show. Its area is about that of Palestine, or a little less than Wales. One cannot wonder that successive Governors of the Madras Presidency have gloried in this gem of their dominions — as the Punjab especially delights in Kashmir. Sir Mountstuart Grant Duff described Travancore as 'one of the fairest and most interesting realms that Asia has to show.' Lord Connemara, the famous, amorous Governor of Madras, called Travancore 'a fairy-land' — and indeed, it has much of that effect. Lord Curzon, who can always write (if not govern) well, speaks of 'its exuberant natural beauties, its old-world simplicity, and its Arcadian charm...In one respect His Highness enjoys a peculiar position and responsibility, for he is the Ruler of a community that is stamped by wide racial differences, and represents a curious motley of religions.'

The little journey here recorded took place in the December of 1907 and the January of 1908. It may be said that I chose the two months which are apt to be the coolest in most parts of India. But in this detail, as in so many other curious ways, Malabar differs from the normal. I was told that I would have found more of an approach to coolness, and a better climate to travel in, if I had entered Malabar a month or two earlier, in November, or even in October, just after the monsoon. Malabar is so charmingly out of the beaten track that the traveller has to find out such facts for himself. Of books upon the subject, at least of any printed and accessible in Europe, there are practically none.

I started from Satara, in the heart of the goodly Maratha country, which is probably the part of India best worth living in. Yet 'The Times' has lately stated that Indian sedition, which shows itself the worst in Bengal, had its origin in Poona, the Maratha capital. The peoples and the States among whom I moved for the next two months were really on the scale of many in Europe, and quite as various. It is, perhaps, hard for the home-keeping Englishman to realise, for example, that the Tamils and the Telegus, two of the peoples only casually mentioned in my text, are as different as the Swedes and the Swiss, and in either case several times as numerous. I stopped for a fortnight in Bangalore, where Mr. Madhava Rao administers a thriving land of the size of Bavaria, or Scotland, or Portugal. A European has called this reformer 'the most dignified native I know.' Another, in Travancore, said that when Madhava Rao ruled that country, you might go to him with a request which he had to refuse, yet be so delightfully received as to leave his presence feeling better pleased than if you had gained your object.

I am glad to be able to present, with this volume, so good a map of Southern India. For me, the little journey has had the result of filling up those fascinating vacant spaces on the map, which finally would not let me rest until I had investigated them. There are things infinitely picturesque and romantic in Travancore, unequalled in the world besides. The ruler of that State is, in a special sense, the King of the Elephants. His is the chief elephant country in India. The elephant is the emblem of his House, which is mentioned even in the Edicts of Asoka. There is no national coat-of-arms quite so expressive as that of Travancore, with its two elephants, ramping on either side of the conch shell which symbolises the sea. I never wearied of watching this emblem, whether upon stationery, or upon the glittering breasts of the peons (footmen).

It is often said that the native sovereigns of India have been reduced to mere shadows. Yet there is a very real feudality left to them. I remember once, when driving through the streets of Trivandrum, how the friend with me suddenly told the coachman to drive down a side street. The Maharaja was coming down the main thoroughfare. By a surviving custom, which is beginning to be resented, all his subjects who may be riding or driving on such an occasion are expected to alight, and to stand humbly by the roadside while he passes. This is the ruler whose image is here presented, in a handsome autograph portrait contributed by himself. Among the things which I have not had space to mention was an entire set of the special coins, and also of the special postage stamps of the country, which was kindly collected for me.

This volume is absolutely without any pretension, save to good faith. I have set down nought in malice. The utmost pains have been taken to reach the truth, and that at first hand, not through the writings of others. Hardly any attempt has now been made to go back upon my impressions, or to correct the praise and the very rare blame which it seemed right to assign at the time, I sincerely trust that no legitimate susceptibilities have been wounded. When I left for Malabar I was assured, by the highest authority, that I would be enabled to see things, in the way of social and family organisation, which no European had ever seen before. I cannot for one moment believe that this happened. Probably the fault was in myself, in that I was unable to see what existed close around me. It is more than Governmental help, with goodwill on the part of the observer, that is required in order to discern many of the peculiarities in a shy and secretive people. There were days when my eyes and my brain ached with the effort of trying to see, yet I felt that the essence of things had escaped me. The special topsy-turvydom of some arrangements in Malabar gives an additional effect as if of standing upon your head.

These Letters, as I have repeatedly said in the course of them, make no pretence of being other than superficial, sometimes hasty, but always honest, efforts to render the strange fleeting impressions which surrounded me during one of the most intense and delightful months of my life. The real Book of Malabar must be written by one (preferably, for the sake of objectivity, a European) who has lived in the country at least twenty years, who knows Malayalam, and the elusive hearts of the Malayalis. There are many such men, but they have not hitherto had time to write.

During the past week I have been carried anew to Travancore by the reading of a couple of volumes. A glance at these will serve to bring the matter of my Letters further up to date. One of them is the 'Brief Sketch of Travancore,' given me at the time by the writer, and mentioned in the text. It is written in an English at once original and spirited, and distressingly printed, like most publications in India. 'The talented pen of Mr. J. D. Rees has covered with additional charm,' we may read here of Travancore, 'its enchanting forest glades and flora.' Of a high wind of the country, we read that through a certain pass 'it rushes forth vehemently, and upsets many a cart and traffic and even men.' Each Maharaja of Travancore, on receiving the coronation sword, has still to declare, 'I will keep the sword until the return of my uncle' — this in reference to the mysterious Perumal who once sailed off across the Arabian Sea. It is rather confusing, in all Malabar writings, to find the use of the Malabar Era, beginning in A.D. 824.

The first English Resident in Travancore, who in 1805 concluded with the Maharaja the Treaty of subsidiary alliance which still holds, was Colonel Colin Macaulay, an uncle of the historian. What would we not give to get hold of the Memoirs which such a man might have written, in the days before the peculiar institutions of Malabar had begun to fade! Equally, the imagination aches for some detailed record of a later Resident, General Cullen, who bore powerful sway from 1840 to 1860, and whose memory is still green in the land. In the text which follows, I have spoken at some length of the sweet little Queens, or Ranis, of Travancore, who, by the way, sent the portraits here printed, with their names upon the back in crabbed, childish English handwriting. I have also spoken elsewhere of a rather rare phenomenon of untaught genius, the painter, Ravi Varma. But I omitted to bring out a connection which I hardly realised. The Brief Sketch shows the fine countenance of the late artist, and states; 'The Ranis are the grand-daughters of the celebrated Indian Artist, Mr. Ravi Varma Koil Tampuran, whose name stands on fame's lofty pinnacle raised by the spontaneous homage of the enlightened aesthetic world.'

The other book is the 'Proceedings of the Fifth Session of the Sri Mulam Popular Assembly of Travancore,' excellently printed at the Government Press in Trivandrum, and lately sent me by the Diwan. This Assembly last met in November, 1908. I missed its previous sitting, by a month or more. The Diwan has been kindly anxious that I should attend it at some time in the future, because of the wonderfully revealing quality of its proceedings. But I am not likely to do so save in the pages of such a Report, which, with some knowledge of the place and the people concerned, quite enables you to see and hear the proceedings. It is a volume of some 125 huge pages. About a fifth part of it is devoted to the Address of the Diwan, or Prime Minister. At the beginning of this I noted, with regret, the death of the gentle Diwan Peshkar of Quilon, towards whom I had come to feel as a friend, after a few interviews. As is mentioned in my text, he was ill the last time I passed through Quilon. Diabetes is, by the way, the characteristic disease of the educated classes in Malabar, who are stated seldom to live beyond the age of forty-five or forty-eight.

The Address shows the hard-headed ability of the writer. There is a guarded reference to the most unusual riots at Trivandrum, in June, 1908, which were doubtless due to Police causes. Two of the members also urge the reform of the Police Department, which is nowhere in India satisfactory, 'It was a regrettable circumstance, that, instead of being the protectors of personal property, the policemen very often assume themselves the position of aggressors....There was at present no security of personal property in the taluk, and the people were spending restless nights.' Again: 'The police obtained bribes for releasing on bail: ...arrested and tortured innocent people, and wrongfully included rich people as accused, with a view to extort some money from them.' For all that, Travancore is happier than most Indian lands. The Police in Kashmir are foully corrupt. Even in the stately fabric of our own rule, the Police make one of the weak, and even dangerous, points.

During his first whole year of rule, the Diwan has converted a large standing deficit into a small safe surplus. All will learn with regret that in Travancore, of all places, in Cocoanutcore, as it has been called, some blight or disease among the cocoanut trees is now upon the increase. Government will do all that European science can teach to combat this. During the past year a separate Department of Agriculture has been founded, under the charge of a young Travancorean, who has returned to his home with a Scottish and with a German doctorate. A substantial improvement is announced in the work of the Land Revenue Department during 1908. Credit is thus given to the Diwan Peshkars and to the Tehsildars, in place of the blame which was awarded them the year before, and which is quoted in my text.

At the first, it rather overwhelms the imagination to think of a Popular Assembly being in full existence in the most remote and primeval of Indian lands. This volume, which permits of being read with interest from cover to cover, can leave no further room for doubt about the civilisation which prevails in Malabar. Yet the constitution and the working of the Assembly show that, however genuinely popular it may be, it is neither legislative, executive, nor widely representative. No such body would for a moment satisfy the demands of the ill-conditioned modern agitators in British India! Not even under the monarchy of Louis Philippe could the franchise have been upon a narrower basis. In order either to elect or to be elected, a person has, essentially, to have a yearly income of 3000 rupees, or £200 — a figure which represents far more in India than in England. With the aid of nominated members, and of some fancy franchises, the number of members may be as high as 100. Last November it was but 82. A member must give notice as to the subject he wishes to speak upon, and no member may speak upon more than two subjects.

The object of the Assembly is defined as being 'to elicit non-official public opinion,' therefore no Government servant can either vote or be returned. The members do not answer each other, still less do they vote, or express any united opinion. In addition to the day devoted to the Diwan's speech, the Assembly sat but for three and a half days last November, Such a thing as an Opposition is not dreamt of. The typical procedure is for a member, less often for several members, to speak briefly; then to receive the Diwan's reply, which is always final. He speaks with great courtesy, but his position is dominating. Sometimes there is an unmistakable ring in the answer, as thus, 'The suggestion to organise a Council to help the Diwan does not commend itself to His Highness' Government.'

Even in urging an expansion of the scope of the Assembly, a member spoke of it as having been 'a spontaneous gift' of the Maharaja. In his reply, the Diwan spoke of the steady expansion which the Assembly had undergone during the four years of its existence, and of the moderation always shown in its deliberations. 'I would strongly advise you to leave the matter there, in His Highness' hands. The authority which brought the Assembly into being may well be trusted to develop it on safe and sound lines.' In his concluding speech, the Diwan speaks of his desire 'to know from the people themselves their wants and aspirations.' The Assembly has already had an important share in regulating the work of the Travancore Government. 'What *does* matter is the recognition by us that questions raised by you *have* to be met.' For the rest, in the course of the proceedings, we see the paltry Mahommedan community, even in Travancore, exhibiting that touchiness in religious matters which is so sure to give offence, but which Moslems have always known how to make superlatively offensive. What troubles them now is the handling of the Koran in courts by non-Mahommedans. 'According to their religious injunctions, even the Mahommedans could not touch the book when they were in a polluted state.'

More serious wrongs, picturesque abuses, 'old, unhappy, far-off things,' upon which we must not here linger, are indicated in representations as to the disabilities of Native Christian converts in the matter of inheritance, and of 'satrom' accommodation when travelling; and specially, as to the disabilities, in the matter of education, of the very large and depressed community of toddy-drawers, known as Elavas, or Tiahs. Such things can hardly be discussed without exciting passionate sympathy; and they once abounded in Travancore. Even at the latest date, the Diwan had to adhere to the decision that the Sanskrit College and another institution must still remain closed to Elavas. Travancore was casually referred to as being, which is undeniable, less orthodox than Cochin. The remedying of such things must be left in the hands of those who best understand them. For very special reasons, in the two Malabar States, it is necessary to remember the old wise maxim about not stirring up the waters of Lake Camarina — *ne quieta movere.*

I have also been reading one of the more recent French books on India, with the strange title of 'Le Mamoul,' by Paul Mimande (Juven). Although several of the very best books about India have been written by Frenchmen, this is a queer book, which is not to be praised. As far as Malabar is concerned, the writer seems merely to have glanced at Mahé, the trivial French settlement on that coast. He is so incredibly slipshod in his mental processes, as actually to mix up the well-known matriarchy of Malabar with the polyandry of the Himalayas, of which, again, he saw nothing at first hand. This is an example of the sort of misconstruction to which the Malabar people are sometimes subjected, and which they have a right to resent bitterly.

The truth would seem to be, that it is as a sex, and not as an individual, that woman holds so strong a position in Malabar. She is honoured and invaluable as the channel of inheritance. But personally, she is a good deal kept under, and by no means allowed, at least in Travancore, all the alleged liberty with which the lascivious imaginations of outsiders have surrounded her. She may escape the domination of her husband, but not the domination of that joint-family system, which, merely modified in a matriarchal sense, is here, perhaps, stronger than anywhere else in India. This system of lifelong family guardianship is expressed by a long word, *Marumakkathayam*, which I have not once used in the text, though it is often seen in the Indian journals. This control, beneficial on the whole, or at least during the past, is exercised, sometimes harshly enough, by an elected head of the family, generally the senior uncle. Against this there has been much recent revolt, as to which I am not competent to judge. The casual traveller, however keen may be his own interest in things seen, ought, in good faith, to try to avoid going beyond his depth, or making rash pronouncements upon matters which are of vital concern to millions of human beings.

My tour through the Malabar States made me acquainted with a far greater number than I could have supposed existed, of descriptive official publications, most of them very well 'gotten-up,' as the Americans say. Not one of these is easily accessible in Europe. While abounding in interesting matter, they are not without the quality of aridity. They are certainly too 'meaty' for most readers, even could these get at them. Pre-eminent among such works is one which I have warmly praised in the text, namely, the 'Travancore State Manual' of my venerable friend Mr. Nagam Aiya. This would be a treasure-house for European ethnologists, if they but knew of it, while it might well pay a London publisher to bring out a reasoned abridgment of it. I was much tempted to double or treble the length of my present volume by adding liberal reductions from Nagam Aiya. But they would have remained accretions. Such a process, while increasing the intrinsic interest of this little volume, would have hurt its unity.

But except for heavy official publications, I have to come back to my original impression, that singularly little, either popular or literary, has been written about Malabar. If such books exist, they have not reached my hands. Of a high literary quality, I know only the quarter part of an otherwise dull book by Loti, and the too few, scattered writings about Malabar which Mr. Rees may some day be persuaded to collect.

In this Preface I have hardly mentioned Cochin. But it will be found to occupy quite its proportionate place in the text. It is a jolly little State, with one formidable drawback. Cochin is rightly proud of being absolutely the most flourishing spot, and one of the loveliest, in all huge India. But it has developed a unique horror in what is often called Cochin Leg (elephantiasis). In contrast to so many Indian States, which are of the size of European kingdoms, Cochin is about as large as an average English county. When the cultured wife of its Diwan was last in England (where she was presented at Court by Mrs. Gladstone), she found it useless to try to make her friends understand the difference between the State of which her husband had just taken charge, and the French Indo-China. The Raja of Cochin is a King of Yvetot, fabulously ancient and sacred, with something of Byzantine pretensions. He would scorn to be called Maharaja (Great Raja), and is really more important than most Maharajas, who are often of yesterday. Equally, the Sire de Coucy was proud of being neither Prince nor Duke; while there are peculiarly swagger English Earls who would not accept a dukedom. Another unique thing about Cochin is its pitiful little community, alleged to be thousands of years old, of White and of Black Jews. These have long had a world-wide renown which they scarcely deserve. That is one of the fascinating things about

Malabar, that within a moderate compass you come upon so many details which are unique or superlative, unmatched in the world besides.

About British Malabar, a land of reputed enchantment, whose fair women, now stated to be largely European in blood, are widely scattered over Southern India, I regret that I can say nothing. During 1908 some attention was drawn to Travancore by the visits of three distinguished guests, the Metropolitan of India, Sir Archibald Hunter, and Lord Kitchener.

I may be allowed to bring still further up to date the vivid little world which I have tried to present in these pages, by quoting a few sentences from a letter just received from Travancore: 'The Diwan prospers, and is doing solid work. His New Year C.I.E. is an acknowledgment of genuine administrative talent, marvellous tact, unfailing courtesy, and untiring energy...The Diwan's "driving power" is felt in every department of the State service, and his vigilance is unsleeping...Mr. V. P. Madhava Rao has had no further honours. He certainly deserves all that the Government could give him, for he is really my highest ideal of an Indian gentleman. There is famine in Mysore, and I do not think he will retire this year, as he intended...Nagam Aiya has turned aged in an alarmingly sudden fashion. He is now a negligible quantity in the eyes of the time-servers of the State. The little Senior Rani has grown into a very charming personage. Her beauty is undeniable. For the rest, we stagnate. Indian Unrest does not concern us.'

The following pages will be found to contain a far larger number of parentheses than would be advisable upon strictly literary grounds. These are chiefly explanations, inserted for the benefit of readers in England, of words or of references which are familiar to Anglo-Indians. It has seemed better to be too explicit rather than not explicit enough — to dot every 'i,' and to cross every 't.' With the same motive, I will here collect a few of the more indispensable explanations. Careless folk in England must, please, by no means confound the words Brahmo and Brahman. A Brahmo is a member of the liberal Brahmo Samaj organisation which has now been happily leavening Indian life for eighty years past. Save for some phases of missionary work, it is the most hopeful thing that India contains, among so many things unhopeful. The word Brahman too often means the very opposite, expressing mere obscurantism. Brahmanism must needs be hated, so far as it connotes priestcraft. But it also, and very often, connotes something which it is hard not to sympathise with, namely, a trained and hereditary intellectualism, which is yet dreadfully given to exploiting all other classes. The word Diwan (often spelt Dewan) means the Prime Minister of a Native State. A Tehsildar is the local subordinate magistrate, with a jurisdiction of a few hundred square miles, who is found all over British and Native India, generally by that name, yet called Mamlatdar in the Bombay Presidency, and Amildar in Mysore. A 'taluka,' or 'taluk,' is the sub-district ruled by a Tehsildar. A Diwan Peshkar, in the Malabar States, is the administrator of a group of a good many sub-districts, and nominally corresponds to a Collector in British territory. An undecorated

British Resident in a Native State can, as I have known in several cases, if it comes to a crisis, forbid a given salute or marriage in the ruling family, or even determine the removal of his powers from a Maharaja. This is the Service, the Indian Political, which (outside of Malabar) is most often accused of harshness and of swollen head.

A rupee, it may be added, is sixteen pence, though practically meaning a good deal more, while fifteen rupees are a pound. An anna is a penny, although, again, signifying more.

Finally, I must renew my thanks to His Highness Rama Varma, G.C.S.I., G.C.I.E., Maharaja of Travancore, who was my host during the greater part of the journey here recorded.

Henry Bruce.

Plymouth, *April,* 1909.

On the Way to Malabar

Pleasant Bangalore: Phases of Indian Life

I HAVE spent ten or twelve days in Bangalore, drinking in information at every pore, yet seeing few of the things which Europeans ordinarily see. I can therefore say little of the European life of the place — nor would it be desired if I could. The trivialities of society will find no record here. But I can no longer wonder at the popularity of Bangalore as a European residence. The air is said always to have a certain quality of coolness, even in April and May. In December it is certainly delicious, distinctly cooler than on the Western side of India. But the coolness always stops short of the point where either great-coats or fire-places are required. Shivering old Anglo-Indians have been known to prefer Bangalore to Ooty (Ootacamund, the famous South Indian sanatorium, on the Nilgiris) as an all-the-year residence, declaring that Ooty is too cold.

Possibly the preference is helped out by the superior cheapness of life in Bangalore. For two great blessings are to be found here, if not three. There is the blessing of comparative cheapness. Of all large and desirable places in India, Bangalore is probably the cheapest. The 'increasing burden' makes itself here felt the least. Such pretty bungalows, both on a modest and on a large scale, can still be had at rates less than those of Western India, greatly less than those of the North. I have heard a man grumbling at having to pay 105 rupees (£7) a month for 'a small house.' On the other hand, something quite decent and attractive can be had for 25 rupees.

But Bangalore is getting congested. About the same proportion holds in regard to servants' salaries. After the West and the North, one is amazed to hear of servants, and good ones, at 6 and 8 rupees (about half a pound) a month. A man from Rangoon tells, in contrast, how ordinary servants commonly cost 22 or 25 rupees. This great blessing of cheapness holds yet more strikingly in regard to native life, about which I intend chiefly to speak.

Then there is the blessing of space. This is a noble blessing. The 13 ½ square miles of Bangalore cantonments are laid out upon a grandiose scale. The roads are avenues. The smallest bungalow has something of a compound. In the larger premises it is a far cry, literally a good walk for an invalid, from the house to the back hedge. The same principle seems to hold in the bungalows. I am astonished at the scale of space allowed, even in the poorer ones — at the height of ceiling, the breadth of rooms. This becomes still more noticeable in the cheap and healthy settlement of Whitefields, 12 miles away, of which I shall speak.

This liberality of scale is not necessitated by the climate, as on the plains of Madras. And it seems to extend even to the native houses, few of which can be called mere huts. Yet a pleasant breeze is almost always blowing over these fair uplands, 3000 feet and more above the sea. It is to be hoped that Bangalore will expand by way of out-settlements, or by any other way, rather than by the sacrifice of her stately spaces. For a Sanitary Commissioner tells me that already things are not as healthy here as they seem, or as they ought to be. There is trouble about the water supply; and a tendency to malaria, as well as to certain epidemics.

Another blessing, allied to that of space, is silence. This is largely explained by the big bungalows and compounds of Bangalore. That most loathsome of all things, the unasked propinquity of one's fellow-creatures, can here be escaped more easily than in most large stations. For propinquity almost invariably means the trouble of noise. Emile Faguet, in reviewing a Life of Beethoven, lately spoke of how many literary men would welcome the deafness which crushed the composer! But in Bangalore there would be the least possible occasion for such flippancy. The measured tramp, tramp, of the big carriage horses sometimes seems rather to beat into one's brain. But there is little else to complain of. The Diwan (Prime Minister) has suggested that the quiet, even of the native city of Bangalore, may be due to the fact that there is no manufacture, and little trade. Even hereabouts the people are mostly farmers. But I have thought to go deeper, and have wondered whether the Canarese people are not naturally quieter than the Marathas.

This is a large question; and, like all questions of race, fascinating. The Canarese, as I shall show, enjoy a larger measure of practical prosperity today than do the Marathas. They are cleaner, quieter, more civil. Yet to be among them increases one's respect, in a way, for the adventurous, far-flung Maratha race. The Maratha Brahman — it is not always a nice type to deal with, nor one loved by British rulers. But to this day much of Southern India is administered, as it has long been, by this type. Out of 20 Diwans, who have governed in Travancore during about a century past, 14 have been Maratha Brahmans. Perhaps we must admit them to have, like the Turks, some natural gifts for organisation and for rule. 'Their faithless dealings with friends and with foes,' says Risley. Oh, well, they have treated me handsomely enough in Mysore State, where also they largely bear rule. The public service is packed with them, specially at the top.

Who, in the native habitat of the Marathas, stops to remember Shivaji's brother Vyankaji, and the colony which he led to Tan j ore? That colony, with its strict endogamy, its clear-cut features, and its light complexion, cherishing Marathi as its family speech, has furnished an indecent proportion of the administrators of the South. At a recent date Marathi was the official language of Mysore. Raja Sir T. Madhava Rao (1828-1891), widely admitted to be the greatest of native administrators, greater even than Sir Sheshadri Iyer, was of that Tanjore colony. The State Government of Mysore consists of the

17

Diwan, drawing 4000 rupees a month, and two Councillors, with less than 2000 rupees each. These three really make the Ministry. The Diwan, Mr. V. P. Madhava Rao, of whom I shall here say little, although he has shown me most that I have seen, is a Maratha Brahman of Tanjore.

The First Councillor, Mr. Ananda Rao, is the only surviving son of Sir T. Madhava Rao. He is, by the way, a literary man. He has rich materials, and hopes, in due time, to bring out such a Life of his father as has never yet been published of an Indian statesman. In contrast the Canarese people seem to be singularly little fitted, as yet, to assert themselves in any way except as cultivators. In Mr. Ananda Rao's house, just now, I saw, for the first time, a good picture of Sir T. Madhava Rao. I was struck with the Hindu quality, and more, of the face. Here was a congener, not exactly of Shivaji, but of the earlier Peishwas and their abler Ministers — of those Poona statesmen, in short, whom Mr. Kincaid has studied.

The foulness of beggary seems to be hardly known in Bangalore cantonments. A word may be said for the old-established Cubbon Hotel, in half a dozen detached bungalows. Its strong point is the big, airy rooms, and plenty of them. The plaster in Bangalore houses, somehow, does not seem to peel off as in Western India. Stucco, here, has almost the solidity of stone. It is said to be due to an admixture of sea-shell in the material. My friends tell me that I ought to be at the swagger hotel of Bangalore, where everything is superlatively up-to-date. But I do not believe I could there have had the same space and quiet.

Mysore State also has the reputation of being superlatively up-to-date. I have heard an Executive Engineer, from a British district, grumbling that the Mysore Government sends its engineers about the country in motors — a really profitable trick, which the British Government has not yet caught on to. On the Bombay side it seems to be beginning to do this, to some degree, for officers whose duties range over many districts.

PLEASANT BANGALORE: A MOTOR INSPECTION

A bright Sunday morning, European weather; a powerful Daimler car, with two genial officers of the State (one of them again from Tanjore). The objective is a typical taluka centre, an admittedly rather favourable specimen. It is called Anikal. It is a town of four or five thousand inhabitants, on the State border, 24 miles from Bangalore. An hour out, something more than an hour there, an hour back. So this is the Canarese countryside! It is 'maidan-mulukh,' in the Marathi phrase which is also used here. It is certainly as pretty as such level country can be. A feature is the beautiful wayside avenues, largely of mango trees. This is a very fertile land, but a little hard-up for water, which is stored in tanks: rivers are somewhat to seek. The road, exquisitely made, passes over a section of Salem district.

Anikal is a widespread town, with ample spaces, humming with quiet prosperity. We alighted at the dispensary, where there was not a single pa-

18

tient. It was a pleasant house in a compound, served by a medical assistant who rises to 60 rupees a month, and by a trained midwife on 15 rupees (£1). That last personage, if widely scattered throughout the Maratha country where she is not liked, might be the means of saving so many lives! On another day, in a village of 1000 inhabitants, I found an equal medical establishment, which served a good many lessor places as well.

On that Sunday morning we were quickly joined by the Amildar, a very young, picked man. In the State there are, in all, 68 Amildars, corresponding to our Mamlatdars or Tehsildars. The pay of their grade ranges from 150 rupees to 250 rupees. An Amildar is a little Raja within his domain of a few hundred square miles. He has therefore many temptations to corruption, which are resisted, not invariably, but on the whole more successfully than by similar officials in British territory. Amildars in Mysore are seldom second-class, and never first-class, magistrates. The standard of uprightness is said to be singularly higher among the corresponding judiciary.

On this occasion we went pretty well over the town with the Amildar, followed at a little distance by a perfectly quiet crowd. I have noticed the great simplicity of the relations here between the officials and the people. They are undemonstrative almost unto baldness, with none of the kow-towing and stand-to-attention expected in many quarters. It probably makes for effectiveness, and for the keeping in touch with the people. The Canarese people are said to be very easy to govern, seldom quarrelling, save rarely when drunk in the evening.

At Anikal the Amildar lived in an excellent house with a wide compound, hired at some absurd rent of 8 or 9 rupees a month; I noticed, as also elsewhere, a feature which the archaeologists may explain. In the centre of the roof is a rectangular opening for the rain water, which is received in a pleasant little tank, of corresponding shape, just below. Is not this what the ancient Romans had, and called 'impluvium'?

Two days later I was taken out in another direction, to a large village called Velahanka. Here we saw, among other things, the village schoolhouse, which had cost 3000 rupees. The girls' school, as always, was the more interesting. In a village of 1000 people, 100 youngsters were attending school, a quarter of them being little girls. The Mysore people are not specially intelligent or literate. In this respect they are behind Travancore, and several British provinces. Their blessings of good rule and of prosperity come to them largely from above, and from outside.

This wonderful system of rule was the work of Englishmen, between 1831 and 1881. But it is stated to be now even better carried on, certainly more cheaply, and perhaps more sympathetically, by Indians. I also hear that even the Model State is slowly swinging back into Indian slackness. This may be true of the larger movement. But, immediately, things are far more efficient now, under Madhava Rao, than they were under his predecessor a few years back.

Running together the impressions of those two days, here are some of the broad results. The Canarese people seem to be greatly more prosperous than their Maratha neighbours. This certainly holds about housing and clothing. I was amazed at the standard of domestic decency and cleanliness among the quite common people, with incomes of 6 or 8 rupees per family: The town and village roads are enormously better than in the Maratha country, and also better, I am told, than in the Tamil country. Every corner of a street or of a courtyard here seems swept. There seem to be none of those offensive sights undeniable in a Maratha village. The humblest Canarese houses look to be human and decent habitations, often with little signs of some money to spare. I could live in some of these houses myself, if brought to it; whereas I would snuff out quickly enough in either a Kashmiri or a Maratha dwelling.

I recall the spacious, clean premises, with a well in the courtyard, of a weaver family, earning in all 25 rupees. A potter's house had many plants in flower-pots before it, with some framed pictures on the walls. Yet the plague enters even here: many houses have been unhappily emptied by death. The Canarese people are neatly, completely, clothed. A naked child is seldom seen. This is only in part explained by the greater cold here. It is an economic fact, which counts for a good deal in Western India, that practically no child under five needs any clothing.

In clothes and in houses the Canarese people are clearly ahead. But they cannot be ahead all along the line. I suspect that they are behindhand in the quality of their food, though they all get a bellyful. The 'bazari' and the 'zondhali' of the Western side make a sweet, if not very digestible, bread, which many Europeans like to nibble at. Neither of these grains is known here. The general food of the people is 'raji,' called 'natsani' in the Maratha country. It is made, not into 'bhakars' or flat cakes, but into balls of varying size. Now, 'natsani' is a rough grain which ordinary people scorn to eat on the Western side. It is there used only by backward people in isolated valleys, and the like.

I failed to get any 'raji' or 'natsani' to taste, though it was promised me. 'Impossible!' was one answer: 'It would mean sudden death.' Another officer says it always gives him diarrhoea to taste 'raji.' Can the inferior physique of the people be due, in addition to their Dravidian race, to such food? This grain now sells at over 30 seers per rupee. Little rice is here eaten. Yet, as one of them remarked, all the Mysore officers are eaters of rice, which is a more intellectual food. Contrast with this Edison's clever remark, made, however, before the Russo-Japanese War: 'If you eat rice, you will think rice.'

Of the looks of the people here there is little room for doubt. The men, carefully dressed, are often decent enough appearing. But the women present an almost total absence of good looks. Many a little girl has a nice face, wholesome and attractive rather than pretty; you would like to get acquainted with her. But she will grow up into a mere Dravidian woman, with twisted features. Yet, as ethnologists have often remarked, there is a certain brief period when even Dravidian girls may have a fleeting charm, due to youthful freshness and good nature. In this land, so highly favoured by nature, the predominance of the Maratha Brahmans almost seems an assertion of racial supremacy. For the rest, sedition is here a distant echo, the meaning of which is hardly grasped. The Mahomedans are now looked down upon where Hyder Ali once ruled. I have noted, and have plainly said, that the rulers of Mysore State, so far advanced in executive and intellectual arts, are socially backward.

The better people here use faultless English, free from the subtle absurdities of Bengal speech: they have no need to fear the shafts of Mr. Anstey. But Hinduism rules here with a harshness and intolerance unknown in the North. I rubbed my eyes, and long could not realise that the Kala Pani superstition (forbidding Hindus to cross the sea) is still vital in South India. It prevented Sir T. Madhava Rao and Ramiengar from visiting England a generation ago: to this day it badgers, if not ruins, many a promising career. The enlightened State must have European training. Young men are expensively supported abroad, and on their return sometimes expelled from caste for it, I must not speak of delightful intercourse with a dozen of the higher State officials. Little oases in the social waste are any Brahmo Samaj families, with the fine, fearless attitude towards life of their often cultured women.

A final motor trip included Whitefields and several orphanages. The orphans are very brown, illustrating the saying: 'God made the native, but Tommy made the Eurasian.' At a large girls' school, nothing was so pretty as the romping delight of some of the boarders in the motor. It absolutely must be brought in, and taken round and round the big premises, until all the girls had had a ride, and many of them several.

Whitefields is on a breezy, barren little plateau, 12 miles from Bangalore, and somewhat higher. It is superlatively healthy, dull and cheap. Near 50 bungalows are occupied exclusively by old pensioners, of a certain grade. Something of a house, with some furniture, can here be had for 15 rupees (£1) a month; a fair house for 25 rupees; a swagger one for 40. One might do worse than end up at Whitefields.

Letters from Malabar

Chapter One - Inland Cochin

'THAT charming land which travellers never visit,' Malabar has been called.

Already I am informed, with regret, that this is beginning to be no longer wholly true. The bloom has just begun to wear off Malabar; but much yet remains. The steps of the globe-trotter proper are as yet almost unknown here. So true is this, that it is well-nigh impossible to get a modern account of Malabar which is at once adequate and popular. Nothing exists comparable to Sir Walter Lawrence's 'Valley of Kashmir.' There seems even to be no good volume of recent travels, such as the delightful book which was directly the means of taking me to Kashmir, Miss Doughty's 'Afoot through the Kashmir Valleys.'

Making a plunge in my ignorance, I paid a pound for this year's (1907) edition of Murray's Indian 'Handbook.' Surely this would give at least a proportionate space to Malabar, and specially to Travancore! I had long been fascinated by the thought of that isolated, sea-washed kingdom, at the opposite end of the continent from Kashmir, with the conch shell for its picturesque emblem. Kerala, the sacred land of palms, the country lifted up, at Heaven's command, from the ocean waves!

'Travancore,' it has been said, 'is a Heaven for the Brahmans, and for all other people a Hell.' It could not be as bad as that. But one had heard from afar of its wild beauty of sea and mountain, its infinitely curious matriarchal system grafted upon Brahmanical institutions, its fair women with their antique freedom of dress and of manner. Several years ago, in the loveliest spot of Kashmir, I had been transported by the poetical and exaggerated account of Travancore in Loti's book with the cheeky title, as I call it ('L'Inde, sans les Anglais'), to which I shall have occasion to recur. In the new Imperial Gazetteer of India, too, there is an inspiring paragraph about Malabar scenery by Sir Thomas Holdich, whom nobody can remember as having visited the country.

Where should one find a reasoned abridgment of this and much more, the wisdom of the wise done up in portable doses, for the use of the foolish, if not in the latest Murray? The book was dearly bought. Incredible as it may seem, the words Travancore and Trivandrum are not once mentioned in it. Hold, I have it! The word 'Trevandnim,' for which I was looking, must be spelt with an 'i,' in the correct modern way, thus: Trivandrum. Alas! even thus it does not exist.

There are 34 routes up and down India given in Murray, including some to places without railways, such as Kashmir. But Travancore is not there. Cochin, where the railway ends, is given, to the extent of two pages. It is apparently the jumping-off place, 'at the wild end of things.' Not only do globetrotters not go beyond, but it is at once evident why not. There are no places for them to stop in. They would not know their way thither, or the way about.

Save as a guest of the State, one would be nowhere in Travancore. Up to the end, with special provision made that I should in any case fall upon a soft mattress, I was nervous about this dropping off from the known world into the unknown. It was the utter strangeness of things in Cochin and beyond, the charming topsyturvydom altogether, that was disconcerting. In vain I was assured that human life went on here as elsewhere, that, for one thing, 'Trivandrum is a much more intellectual place than Bangalore.' The passing strangeness remained. It was much the same the first time I went to Kashmir, though here there was no such arduous journey involved.

At Podanur, in the morning, I had to change into the Calicut train, though some one, at Bangalore, had promised me I should not have to change, and had put my name up over the window for vain security. Up to Podanur, which is also the station for the Nilgiris, the journey is quite commonplace, over the Madras plains. But very soon beyond, I looked out and saw a wild little mountain with an unmistakable corkscrew twist at the top. 'What range of hills is this?' I asked. 'These are the Western Ghats.'

Exactly; I had not realised how far West, we had come during the night, nor how narrow the Peninsula is here. These were the same weird and unique contortions which I so greatly admired in the same range 500 miles to the North. The hills fall apart at Pal Ghat, for a breadth of some 20 miles, to allow the passage of the trains, and of an occasional invading army. From Olavakot the beginning of Malabar is reckoned.

The change in scenery is instantaneous. I had never seen this sort of thing before. Here is the legitimate conclusion, a good deal more tropical, of the Bombay side Konkan. Great clumps of bamboos, of other luxuriant feathery trees, but above all of palms. 0, that first sight of the crowded palms of the true South! Well might Loti call this 'the India of the great palms.'

Here, and throughout Cochin, I noted that the extreme luxuriance was everywhere held in hand. It is never uncontrolled, it nowhere degenerates into jungle. The neatness of the packed landscape, of the roads, of the dainty little bungalows which are in reality native houses, is wonderful. 0, but those abounding palms! 'All the hairs of thy head are numbered,' used to be said of them in Bombay. The palms are not numbered here. In my life I had not seen so many as I saw that forenoon.

There is such a thing as British Malabar, though we are apt to lose sight of the fact. I was reminded of it last year by a pleasant man who was encamped

23

beside me in Kashmir. He used to insist on my visiting the country, with the life of which he was greatly in love. Yet the only Malabar he knew was the British districts. At Shoranur the line divides. The regular train proceeds northwards, 'all along the delectable Malabar Coast,' as Sir George Birdwood writes. I must reserve that golden shore for the end of this trip, or for another trip. Murray gives it a scant three pages in all.

This, again, was all the Malabar known, and that only during some sorrow-laden months, to the late Mrs. Nicolson (writing as Laurence Hope, author of 'The Garden of Kama'), the finest poetical genius ever produced in Anglo-India, who, I am glad to note, is looming more widely appreciated with each year that passes. My companion in the train was returning from six months in Germany to the charge of some tile works at Feroke, some 7 miles south of Calicut. He remembered the charming bungalow on a hill-top which General and Mrs. Nicolson occupied at Feroke early in 1904, the last year of their lives. Thus the poet wrote of the Malabar people:

'These are my people, lithe-limbed and tall:
  The maiden's bosom they scorn to cover.
  Her breasts, which I shall call and enthrall her lover,
  Things of beauty, are free to all.'

Perhaps the outstanding fact, which begins to be observable on the southward journey from Shoranur, is more conveniently expressed in verse than in prose.

One slips imperceptibly into Cochin State, on a narrow-gauge railway somewhat resembling the Southern Mahratta. The carriages are not so well built, but the speed is better. From Shoranur to the terminus, at Ernakulam, is 65 miles. About a third of the way down is the fair and thriving city of Tri-chur, with 16,000 inhabitants, where I alighted for a day. The scenes at the little wayside stations, the glimpses of homesteads and of people from the carriage windows, were full of interest. A country cultivated like a kitchen-garden, wide expanses of green rice-fields, crowded clumps and groves of bamboos and palms, yet the neatest roads and houses. Everything is hum-ming with prosperity, and with an intense life which, for one thing, seems to conduct itself without much noise. This intensive cultivation must resemble parts of Japan, yet there seem to be no smells connected therewith.

The Malabar heat is not gross or apparent. It is more hidden and inward, yet undeniable. It says with an imperative voice: 'Take off that coat!' The sun does not burn from brazen skies. There are pleasant clouds, and breezes which seem cool. I am told that the Malabar climate is letting me down easy, since I have been able to sleep well for two nights without mosquito nets.

Chapter Two - Trichur

IF there is anything I despise, it is the having to travel, especially in a strange country, without a servant to take care of me. But, in the Scripture phrase, I feared a fear, and it came upon me. At Bangalore I had sent back a helpless creature from the Maratha country. In his place I took, for the Malabar trip, a competent elderly man who had been bearer to Mrs. Bullock Workman the year before. If these lines meet her eyes, she may remember Bob Antony. But at Trichur, for uncertain reasons, he failed to alight from the train.

I had painfully to collect my things, and proceed to the Travellers' Bungalow in a 'jutka.' This vehicle, which I had never entered before, was a smartly varnished springless affair, very neat though rather small, shaped like the old-fashioned bullock 'damani,' but drawn by a pony. The fare for a short distance is only 4 annas (fourpence): prices, though locally rising, are perceptibly lower in these parts. The next day I noticed the driver, squatting at his pony's head, feeding him with handfuls of deliciously fresh grass, taken from inside the jutka. There are hereabouts constant little pleasant touches to life like that. The common people evidently lead a good life, by no means uncivilised.

I had a proof that day of how far Malayalam civilisation may surpass the vaunted product of America. Bob Antony held the key of my box — though I held his testimonials, of which he had said: 'They are my life.' In the noontide, which was clouded, and not apparently very hot, I walked to the station again, not far away, to send a vain telegram about him. It is said, however, not to be wise to take such liberties with the Malabar climate: they may give you a headache later, or worse.

The Travellers' Bungalow is a clean-flagged building, in a shaded courtyard, though quite in the native town. Here I noticed one of the things which may be dispensed with in the Far South. The best houses do not need, and often do not have, any glass windows. But these are said to be desirable in the monsoon, which is commonly of 125 inches. The messman suggested that he should send for the local locksmith. An ordinary-looking native was brought in, half naked. He was the blacksmith and shoesmith, making 30 or 35 rupees a month. In a trice he had opened the padlock which was easy enough. But he took it away with him, and in a few hours sent back an excellent neat new key, better than the old one. The charge, which I was ashamed to pay, was 4 annas!

Contrast with this Kipling's experience, who landed at San Francisco about 1890 with some trifling thing wrong with the lock of his trunk. It took half a pound to have this mended; and the point is that it could not be done without the characteristic incivility of the West.

In the late afternoon and early evening I walked abroad alone, for a couple of hours, through the far-stretching rural town of Trichur, an accretion of villages, as it seemed to be. I know not how to express in a paragraph, which is all that is at my disposal, the impression of comfort, cleanliness, aesthetic life and surroundings which I received. That walk must stand in memory with my first impressions of Baramula, the entering-place for Kashmir. I do not wish to detract from the vivid impressions of the uniquely lovely Kashmir landscape. The Cochin landscape, however, is equally unique, and hardly less lovely. But it was in the people that I felt the difference. The Malabar people are said to seem less nice as you know them better. But what a contrast to the Kashmiris, particularly in their attitude towards Europeans! How much more self-respecting these people seemed! how much less cringing and suspicious! how much less basely 'on the make'! I noticed none of those sights of offence, common in Kashmir and in most Indian lands. Even the pariah dogs were few. The beautifully made roads, of reddish soil, were swept to the last inch, and so were the courtyards. For one thing, the people here have windows, and use them.

There are two outstanding observations. First, as to colour. This is no land of black people. Not a touch of the negritic, so far. The people at Trichur average quite as fair as those in a Maratha town, perhaps more so. They are a light, rather than a dark, brown. I saw three or four women's faces of extraordinary and unexpected beauty, delicately refined. There was breeding there. The people are said to have a Dravidian basis, with a much larger Brahmanic admixture than is admitted. Well, 'thy fault was not thy folly!'

The second point is the high level of popular prosperity. Such pretty little houses, 'coquettish,' as the French say. They may be insanitary, like the houses of European peasants; but how much it is to be able to make that comparison! I noticed a score of little bungalows in which I should be glad to live myself, except, perhaps, for the crowded neighbourhood. There were several bungalows better than I shall ever live in — one large one surrounded by a white-pillared verandah; another behind iron railings joined to massive stone structures. Who lives there? Hindus, without exception. Now, hardly any pleaders or rich natives live on that scale, with that neatness, on the Bombay side of India.

The houses of the poorest seem to be more than tolerable human habitations. Often they are built of reddish stone, suggesting that at Mahableshwar (the sanatorium of Western India, on the Ghats). They are often lit by lamps made in Germany, as good as those in the Travellers' Bungalow. A house just opposite has a much better lamp, with a gay red shade: the man occupying it earns 100 rupees a month. Nowhere, a chance European Customs officer told me, is so much kerosene oil consumed as along this coast. The palms and bamboos are everywhere in the heart of Trichur.

'The people, though quiet, simply swarm, suggesting an overflowing population. For the rest, Trichur is a sacerdotal place, with some overweening pretensions. I was not sorry, on the whole, to miss those super-sacred temples (only the outer walls visible to the profane) from which Loti was waved off with such a memorable gesture of Brahmanic insolence. It was the embodiment of caste. For from the Latin 'castus' come both 'caste' and 'chaste.' 'Get away from me! I'm so pure!' It is a gesture not unknown to Christian priests as well.

In the evening Bob Antony found his way to me, promising never to do such a thing again. All day he had wandered in the heat, with nothing to eat but water. 'It is jungle land,' he said. Ah! my friend, whatever else Cochin may be, it is precisely not jungle.

Trichur has been made his residence by Albion R. Banerji, the young Curzonian Premier of the State, just this week absent in Madras. At the station the next noon I noticed a peon with a broad belt and badge, who soon after noticed me. He had been sent from Ernakulam, with a letter handsome in every respect, from one of the three European officers there resident in the employ of the Cochin State. They make a happy family, fraternal in their relations to all accredited strangers.

I read: 'Mr. Banerji wrote to me yesterday to do all I can for you in his stead. — The Tehsildar of Alwaye, Travancore, is lying in wait for you. He has a cabin-boat ready for you, special relays of rowers, etc.' As the train passed through Alwaye, in Travancore territory, the Tehsildar (local magistrate), to be sure, boarded it. He had been ordered to attend me while I remained in Ernakulam and British Cochin. I must write more about this attentive Tehsildar. But I have persuaded him to return to his charge for a few days, until I can rest and form plans. These confounded letters take such a lot of time: my friends can hardly understand it.

One man, whose name I did not know that morning, had asked me to dinner. Another took me off to his house to stay. Then, casually: 'I don't believe I heard your name!' That is the kind of hospitality which one reads of rather than experiences — 'the grand old Roman way' of doing things. I cannot write here about Ernakulam, with its queer climate and delicious sea front. I return to Trichur to meet the Diwan (Prime Minister).

Chapter Three - Ernakulam and Trichur

AT the end of my second chapter on Malabar I was only able to speak, in connection with Ernakulam, of the fine hospitality, unknown in larger centres, of its few European officers. The view, too, is fine, and unmatched in its sort. It is far more than a mere view over the ocean. Two and a half miles across the backwater is the wooded spit or peninsula of British Cochin and Matanchery, running pretty parallel for most of the way. In the nearer foreground, not a mile away, is the luxuriant little island of Balghatty, containing one of the loveliest Residencies in India. Between the two may be seen glimpses of the real ocean, with half a dozen ships hanging motionless on the horizon. But all this decoration seems to set out the sunsets and the sea, even as a picture-frame adds to the best picture.

The backwater is said to be five or six feet deep. It is evidently clean water, being renewed by internal currents. And up and down its smooth surface glide the boats of the country, sometimes poled, but more often rowed. It is the magic of moving craft, though not exactly of moving water, as in Kashmir. For a note of difference, the thronging palms here reach to the sea.

I was enchanted with the seaward view by moonlight. I was more enchanted in the morning, when I saw the boats slipping silently past the palm trees. So much so, that I thought of hiring the adjoining compound; and began inquiring about house-rents from my attendant Travancore Tehsildar. Some of the figures given were absurdly low; yet I gather that adequate houses for Europeans are few in Ernakulam. A European seeking a house, apart from official necessities, is even more rare. But it was a day before I could surrender the dream.

The view reminded me of the title of Mrs. Nicolson's exquisite poem, 'Palm Trees by the Sea' — though the setting there is evidently Karachi. But, O these palm trees in Cochin! I have always thought that there were two pleasant signs of a bad climate — palm trees and punkahs. Wherever palms flourish it also means the nuisance of an overflowing populace. I have been seriously told, by one of those best entitled to know, that two or three palm trees, with some fish from the backwater, will support a common family through the year. The merchants are now pushing yet another raw product of the fruitful palm, with uses unsuspected a few years ago. This is copra, from which is made cocoatine, a substitute for butter. It is a sort of unearned increment, increasing the wealth of all who own palm trees. Cochin has never known a famine.

Remembering also the peculiar Malabar customs, what check can there be on the population? It simply swarms. It is a better population than most, decent and docile. But it is too numerous. I have trouble in getting away from people and houses for a free stretch into the country. No wonder. By the last census the population in two of the Cochin talukas (sub-districts) averages some 1500 per square mile, and in another near 2000! At the same time the people live in separate homesteads, never huddled together. The climate, too, is undermining. There is an inward heat, as the Tehsildar tells me, though it may seem outwardly cool and airy. He also tells of a 'sulphurous' quality, whether in the air or the water, which helps to account for the special good looks of many of the girls along this coast.

But I am warned of the Malabar Head. This does not connote what the Sind Head (an expression sometimes used for provincial cocksureness) connotes. It means essentially forgetfulness. 'You'll begin to feel it here,' said one, sharply tapping his forehead. For another symptom of Malabar Head: 'It's bad enough to be a fool; but to "feel that you are one!!' This does not apply to the natives, who are acute enough, but to immigrants. The wife of a Collector of Malabar District is recalled who, wishing to sign her name after writing a letter, could not possibly remember what it was. Animals degenerate rapidly along this coast, specially horses. I must return to Ernakulam, in subject and in person. On the day I left I was pointed out, under shelter at Balghatty, the cabin-boat from Trivandrum, which had been awaiting me a fortnight. To-day, at Trichur, I hear of the arrival of Professor Macdonell, the Oxford Sanskrit scholar.

After three days at Ernakulam, I have returned for three days with the Diwan at Trichur. This city, 44 miles to the northward, and inland, is reputed to be the oldest in Malabar. It is the most central place in the little Cochin State, the most convenient for administrative purposes, and greatly the healthiest. Several Heads of Departments are already located here. Trichur ought manifestly to be the capital; but this cannot be for a long time to come, because of the handsome range of Public Offices already existing at Ernakulam. The Diwan has taken up his dwelling at a noble old Residency building, a mile or so out of Trichur. This is nicer than the Travellers' Bungalow, which I did not dislike; but I must say much less about it.

About Mr. Banerji, also, it is because I could write so much that I ought to write but little. Within this year, at least, it has become no novelty to Mr. Banerji to be written about. As the son-in-law of Mr. K. G. Gupta, of the Indian Council, by his own personality, and as the first I.C.S. man appointed to a Diwanship, he has attracted an amount of attention which would have turned many a head. He is obviously of a different caste from any man who has previously held such a post. The amount of matter printed about his work this year would fill a good-sized volume.

How shut up we are in our watertight compartments in India! I am told, at a rough guess, that not one Englishman in 8000 ever gets really in touch with Indian life. With every desire to know, it was not until last year that I was asked to my 'first Parsi tea.' It was only a fortnight ago that I was asked to my 'first Brahmo dinner.' This Brahmo Samaj movement seems to be greatly the most promising in India — pity 'tis that it moves so little of late. 'You were surprised to see that Indian women could eat like that,' a cultured Hindu chaffed me. Ah, that is a trivial matter! It was the fine fearless attitude towards life of the Brahmo women that charmed me, as shown even in the portraits of young girls. To watch girls and young men laughing and chaffing with each other — and already used to this for several generations past — how revolutionary to conservative Indian sentiment!

To note the spirit of culture which prevails among many Brahmo women is to feel that here is something better than mere high education. I am told that there are hundreds of families of much the same culture, if not the same position, as several families which I have seen lately. It is an amazing, unknown, almost unsuspected, world. It hardly exists outside of Bengal; and its weakness is that it includes so few poor people. But with so much that is discouraging in modern India, Brahmo families are surely the salt of the earth, 'Without whom,' in Shelley's phrase, 'the world would smell like what it is, a tomb.'

Mrs. Noliny Banerji is a lady of social charm and of literary aptitudes. She is a member of the Royal Asiatic Society. At present she is engaged in writing a 'History of the Jews in India.' I am anxious to see her reveal to the world, in the form of stories and novels, the unsuspected and interesting life of the Brahmo community.

The Diwan's father, Mr. Sasipeda Banerji, has been a lifelong devoted leader in all the good work of the Brahmo movement. In 1870 he broke the record by taking his family to England. His wife was thus the first Indian lady, certainly the first Brahman lady who ever crossed the bitter Black Water. At Bristol, in the following year, was born her youngest child, named after 'sea-encircled' Albion. It is a fact which Mr. A. R. Banerji has never lost sight of, and which has been a continual source of inspiration to him. He also shared the inspiration of Jowett's last year at Balliol.

It was at a pecuniary sacrifice that, after twelve years in the; Civil Service, he came to Cochin. At thirty-six, he has still the best part of his life before him. His friends, at least, dream for him that he may infuse a new spirit into several Native States. He would like to end his career as a Member of Parliament, where no native I.C.S. man has yet sat. He has a chance to solve an interesting racial question, by showing himself a great Bengali administrator.

Bengalis used to do well at administration long ago. In the recent past, two at least of them, Mr. Dutt and Mr. Gupta, out of only about twenty in the Civil Service, have done notably. With an exception or' two, all these twenty are Brahmos. Mr. Banerji believes, by the way, that by another two years all the unrest in Bengal and elsewhere will have passed like a bad dream. He hopes, long hence, to publish a Life of his father, for which there are interesting materials. Meanwhile, he says: 'I hope to serve my country. For I look upon India as my country; as England is also my country.'

Chapter Four - Under the Palms

UNTIL within these nine days past, I never realised the meaning of the words 'Under the Palms.' It is a stock phrase to compare a lithe, or a straight, young beauty to a palm tree. But palms are more often contorted in various picturesque shapes, which it is a fascination to watch. They are not to be called crooked, but suggest certain famous prints.

To sit by moonlight in one's own compound, beneath nothing but palms, beside a neat sea-wall overlooking, not exactly the ocean, but rippling salt water! 'Have you ever tasted toddy?' A man is sent forthwith up the nearest palm — which is, I am informed, a serious offence against the Excise. 'Do you still wonder at the number of popais on the palm trees?' chaffs another. The allusion is to a blunder, which cannot be infrequent: the bunches of green cocoanuts have a strangely familiar look to those who may know only the homely, useful popai. The fresh toddy, when served in glasses, is a whitish liquid, suggesting uncommonly crude cider, but with further stomachic possibilities. We none of us know what we may come to; but I am not likely to fall a victim to the toddy habit.

Prom around the corner comes, at incalculable hours, a clashing of cracked bolls, and sometimes the firing of cracked cannon. It is a damnable nuisance. It is from 'the Christian temples,' as one has called them. There seems to be no legal remedy. It is here the immemorial custom for Christians of sorts to worship God by letting off contemptible artillery.

I started to write, in praising Cochin State, that here 'you need not fear the cold.' But I am medically informed that even here, within 10 degrees of the equator, you do need to fear the cold. Pneumonia is common. In no season of the year is it safe to sleep outdoors, on account of the heavy dews. In Trichur, for three nights, I had my first experience of sleeping under a punkah. This may seem truly luxurious, particularly if the punkah be some ten feet in length. Other people do not care for a night punkah, saying that it gives them colds, etc.

Trichur is elevated some five or six feet above the sea. Even that absurd elevation distinctly counts. One has a curious sensation of going up towards it. Trichur is not tonic, but you can at least work there. The whole machinery of State Government seems destined to be gradually moved thither. In Ernakulam, as the Diwan says, 'you feel like a worm.' I have not yet experienced quite that; there is always the delicious view, and breeze. What Cochin would be without this breeze is a question which need not be considered.

I hear, by the way, of the conjugal misfortune of the specially stupid servant whom I sent back from Bangalore. Arriving home unexpectedly in the night hours, he found — exactly what might have been expected. Now, I gather that in Malabar such incidents are no misfortune; husbands have no right to resent them. The people here are sensitive, not about having their special customs discussed, but about having strangers seem to cast blame upon them — which I am far from doing. These customs may well be an ideal means for making the most of the race.

My wonder at the apparent level of popular prosperity is not diminished. One has constant glimpses of interiors that ourselves might get along with — neat compounds, lamps, furniture, pictures on the walls, even hat-racks! Nair houses, I am almost always told. How can the people afford it? They seem to score, economically, in at least two respects. Naked natives lounge about these nice houses: their clothes cost little. They seldom keep servants. And their food is simple and inexpensive. Nowhere else in India does there exist a standard of expenditure and of general prosperity.

To complement this fact is another cheerful fact. The richer classes in Malabar never live with any extreme show or extravagance, or greatly above the popular level: they do not incline to castles and retainers. This is another truly democratic consummation. It reminds one of New Zealand (with about the same population as Cochin, 800,000), where the State seeks to have no poverty-stricken citizens, and no very rich ones. In Cochin, I am told, there is some real distress, though not very evident on the surface.

Just a few observations on some institutions in Ernakulam, which I shall not describe. The Diwan, in accordance with his policy of general thoroughness, wishes to see the Ernakulam College the very best second-grade college in the Madras Presidency, before he tries to make it a first-grade one. It dates from 1845, for twenty years following which date it was under the charge of a Mr. Kelly, 'whose salary, it is interesting to note, never exceeded Rs. 45.' I wish that the present Principal could be persuaded to publish some quaint letters and other documents of this Kelly, which would make a revealing study in the Eurasian life of half a century ago.

The Public Offices are the chief impediment to the removal to Trichur. They contain whole rooms full of neat but rather friable revenue records on palm-leaf slips, dating back not much more than a century. The best typewriters have now succeeded all that. My name, with that of the 'Times of India,' was cleverly done for me with a stylus, as a visiting card, in Malayalam.

The jail here is quite shamelessly clean and comfortable, even luxurious. The worst of mankind have indulgences which most honest men lack: the smell of the curry which was being cooked for them made my mouth water. Here, by the way, are, or lately were, two little girl prisoners who would be better with their mothers, or in a Reformatory.

Finally, the admirably conducted general hospital is on a larger scale than many a District Centre hospital in British India, while costing much less. This is often the case in Native States. The hospital made me realise anew how much better such relief is given by those who work for humanity, doing their secular duty, than by those who have an axe to grind, working for some deity or dogma.

Approaching the outside of the Trichur temples the other evening, under due Brahmanic guidance, I was yet waved off from a distance. A little more, I was told, and a wire might have gone to the Raja, saying that the temples were polluted, and claiming some thousands of rupees for the purification ceremonies. In such an event the Diwan would have had to sanction the expenditure. The State spends two lakhs a year on its temples, and on what Froude calls 'the representatives of the imaginary Powers.'

There is a Mongolian touch both in some of these people and in some of their bulging, bulbous architecture. This touch is called either Chinese, or Burmese, or merely Buddhistic. I have even been told that the Nairs may have come from Nepal.

No light can be thrown on this subject by the Boden Professor of Sanskrit, Mr. Macdonell, who was here until to-day. It was a treat to talk about Oxford associations with him. He was born in India, in Tirhut. Within these two months he has learned, as his predecessor, Monier Williams, could not do, to talk Sanskrit fluently with the pundits. Mr. Macdonell thinks it a mistake for a Sanskrit Professor not to visit India. His own knowledge of his subject will now be richer and more real. But India has not yet made him change any points of view. He is trying to arouse the scholarly Raja of Cochin to a systematic search for Sanskrit MSS. and inscriptions. I go over the water to British Cochin, with my friends, this evening.

Chapter Five - A Day in British Cochin - The White Jews

I CAN understand now why the inhabitants of the island of Bombay, until much less than a century ago, used to speak quaintly of the neighbouring mainland as 'the Continent.' That is just the effect which the Cochin mainland has, seen from the long spit or peninsula wherein are situated British Cochin and Matanchery. The spit has all the effect of an island, with quite the isolation. One of the many nuisances of the place is the lack of roads and communications. It is hard to get a walk; while the richest Europeans in the place do not need to keep carriages.

A far more dreadful deprivation must be the absence of drinking water. It seems incredible, but for centuries all the drinking water used by Europeans has been brought from Alwaye (the seat of my attentive friend, the Tehsildar), 12 miles away, in Travancore territory. I believe that when the British took over Cochin, they entered into an engagement to supply the Dutch inhabitants with decent water. The oldest inhabitant of Cochin to-day carries precaution so far as to drink only rain water collected by himself. Soda-water, too, which is not nearly so nice as the natural fluid, has to be largely consumed in order to avoid water, sometimes even to wash your teeth with!

A hideous penalty attends the neglect of these troublesome precautions. It is 'the curse of the country,' or, as I call it, 'the local horror,' elephantiasis. I am not going to talk about this loathsome affliction, just as I have avoided sending any photographs to illustrate it. Happily, I have managed to see but few cases. But to think that this extreme penalty should attend upon dirt in only this odious little section of earth! It is not absolutely unique. The same disease, there called neither elephantiasis nor Cochin Leg, is found both in Samoa and in Barbados. But to think that in Matanchery every second person, or 50 per cent of the population of, I believe, some 20,000, should have it! It is found, also, in some neighbouring tracts of Travancore, but with nothing like the same concentration.

Why should its habitat be so very limited? Modern science can make no answer on the subject, can offer no remedy but the knife, cannot even agree as to the cause of the disease. It is positively stated to be due both to a special mosquito, and to some germ in the local water. Anyhow, the stories I had heard of elephantiasis, from Bangalore on, had got upon my nerves. In vain I was assured that Europeans were immune, at least when they did not live piggishly. The case of some Capucin monks is the only one known, besides that of a former Civil Surgeon of British Cochin. But this was the reason, in addition to the attractions of the mainland, why I gave but a single day out of ten to Cochin.

The people of British Cochin rightly insist upon a difference being made between it, with its two windswept square miles at the end of the little peninsula, and miasmatic Matanchery behind it. Cochin is sultry, but it has the infinite glory of the open sea. I was rowed across the three miles or so from the mainland, with two friends, in a small boat wherein one could recline in a long chair. Here was the open ocean at last, with its salt breath; here were Hamburg liners and others, up to 7000 tons; here were native coasting craft, called 'patamas,' more or less illustrating the perilous ships in which Columbus, and the early English mariners, crossed the Atlantic. I was wild, for a moment, to abandon the Malabar trip, to board the nearest liner, and be taken wherever it might be going!

Even by moonlight Cochin had a curious and delightful effect, as of Holland near the equator. The Dutch, who succeeded the Portuguese and the odious Inquisition, were here from 1663 to 1796. They have left a good memory of themselves — a colonising race to whom justice has never been done!

I was taken to the Club, and given a bedroom. Then: 'Won't you come to my house?' asked a man whose name I had not clearly caught. Before Bob Antony could get used to his bearings, he and I were transferred to the reputed best house in Cochin, the residence of old Dutch Governors, with the sea encircling two sides of it.

'In the Roar of the Sea' — that is the phrase by which I shall recall those twenty-four hours in British Cochin. The next day was powerfully sultry; and even in such a house, with its vast chambers and its floors of cool, slate-coloured cement, I felt the heat as never on the mainland. But O! the thunder and the breeze and the foam of the sea! It might compensate for much. In the verandah, almost overhanging the sea, I was fascinated by the rhythmic movement of the great China fishing nets.

Cochin can contain few of what Heine calls 'consolations for poverty.' There is, by the way, a discreditable pest of beggars. Quite near to the house where I stayed is the finely simple church. Portuguese, Dutch, English, where the body of Vasco da Gama reposed for a few days in 1524. It is the most restful place of the kind I have been into in India, with the green light from some hand painted windows. And there is a legendary grandeur in the association with Gama, by far the most modem man who has inspired anything approaching a first-class epic.

Between the church, and the house in the sea, is the house of Captain Winckler. I am not mentioning people by name, save in the case of public

34

characters. But Captain J. E. Winckler is a public character. All agree that not to know him is not to know Cochin even a little. And none can know Cochin as he does. He is now seventy-five, representing the third European generation of Wincklers in the place. His grandfather was born in the middle of the eighteenth century, in Schleswig-Holstein, and came out in the Dutch service. His father was the last man in Cochin who could decipher a Dutch paper or inscription. Captain Winckler's mother was a Jewess from the too famous Jew Town close by.

He is still an upstanding man, with keen eyes and a flowing beard. He has had eighteen children, who are now settled over the world, from Japan to Chile. One is both a legal and a medical officer at Demerara: one is a Professor at Hanover. Captain Winckler received a scanty education in Bombay, going to sea in 1846. For thirty-one years following, 'bitter years' he calls them, he sailed the seas, having got his first ship only seven years after he began. Then, for sixteen years, he was Port Officer in various places, ending with Cochin. During twenty-two voyages to China he long ago acquired a collection of China ware, the value of which an ignorant person like myself cannot begin to estimate, but which Governors have envied. Captain Winckler's conversation is racy, his memory still vivid. He really owes it to the world not to let all this pass with him.

There could not have been a better guide than Captain Winckler to Jew Town, where I also had another introduction. I have had special reason, in the past, to admire the Jewish race. But it never would have become admirable from such specimens as are content to vegetate in odious Matanchery. The place itself somehow suggests the odour of stale mutton. 'Is it not one of the vilest places on earth?' I asked. 'It is vile,' the Captain corrected; 'but less vile than some other places, for example, Canton and Bushire.'

The road to Matanchery, two miles, is through putrid cocoanut plantations, with mean houses, no longer pretending to the neatness of the mainland. The Excise, by the way, is a nuisance; you may not go shooting for the day across the frontier, taking a few bottles of beer with you, without being liable to arrest. The Black Jews I did not see, nor care to. The White Jews inhabit less than one furlong of a squalid lane. Yet some of the houses reach deep back into cocoanut groves, admitting of a sort of twilight comfort, which must be intensely unhealthy and depressing. In the doorways I saw some children's faces, with the Jewish prettiness, but so dark that I could not believe that they called themselves white.

In the common little synagogue, at the end of the lane, a score of men were screeching their evening prayers, making the most hideous discord, merely vocal, that I have ever heard. 'O! how I hate every kind of orthodoxy!' as another friend refreshingly remarked that day. It is orthodoxy, plus idleness, which is keeping this paltry community in the mud. It is stated to number no more than 100 — a figure perhaps not possible, and only possible with cruel inmarrying.

Then we spent an hour in the spacious interior of the richest family, with lakhs' (a lakh of rupees = £6,666) worth of palm groves in Travancore. I hesitate to speak of these people, since they received us with courtesy; yet they knew for what I had come. The Jews are as liable to elephantiasis as any natives. Their fatalistic attitude on this point is repellent: they find the horrid disease inconvenient, but do not dread it as Europeans do. Here were some little girls with brown hair, with eyes showing the mystery but not the genius of the race, with refined anaemic faces, speaking only Malayalam, yet not timid like native children.

For the credit of the community, I was not allowed to see its poorer members. As Captain Winckler says: 'Every monkey praises his own tail.'

Chapter Six - The Voyage to Quilon

THE Principal of the Ernakulam College, fulfilling to the last the charge laid upon him, saw me aboard by a glorious moon, one day beyond the full. I must mention now or never that the same mentor had Pierre Loti in charge for four or five days just eight years ago, conducting him to Trichur by the troublesome backwater route, which was the only one before the railway. Loti was then pretty well done up, what with the heat and his somewhat rapid progress northward. He is remembered by several as a thoroughly smart officer in appearance, very small and dapper. He is believed to have understood a good deal of English, though he professes an entire ignorance.

Following in his footsteps, though in the opposite direction, I have piously collected recollections, not all of which I can print, of one of the most literary (must I also say affected?) figures that have ever passed through India. In the beautiful Quilon Residency, whence I write. Loti is also remembered. I realise, as his narrative hardly enables one to do, to what a degree his progress was from Residency to Residency. I have heard language, far stronger than is just, as to his conduct in affecting to ignore the English who did so much to make him comfortable.

There is now, to my astonishment, steamboat communication along near 100 miles of the legendary Travancore lagoons. A boat will take you, for a few annas, or for no more than two rupees first-class, from Cochin to Alleppey. Thence another boat goes on to Quilon. The boats are fairly quick, but must be hot enough. Professor Macdonell, being in some haste, had gone on by this democratic method; and by to-morrow (Christmas Day) will have left Travancore.

So he took the 'dhuma-nauka,' as the steamboat is called in modem Sanskrit. But I wanted to experience the traditional method of navigating these backwaters, which may not endure so very much longer. For all but three weeks a cabin-boat from Trivandrum had been awaiting me, with a 'serang,' the 'Admiral' or boatswain, but fortunately not with the entire crew, as I was several tunes informed. The Tehsildat. of Alwaye had the crew engaged, and everything ready, by the evening I had indicated. He tells me, by the way, that his 'taluk,' which cuts in from behind, dividing Cochin territory, has an area of 100 square miles, with a population of some 76,000. The result will indicate the density of population hereabouts, exceeding that of Bihar. The parts of Cochin not covered by forests actually support 1000 inhabitants per square mile.

My cabin-boat has given me, with all differences, a more vivid idea of what galleys must have been like, not only in the classic world, but in parts of the Mediterranean until barely two centuries ago. It is to be noted that these Travancore craft are not called houseboats. In vain I had dreamed of renewing, upon these poetical waters, the experiences of Kashmir. The boats here are not comfortable enough to live upon permanently; and probably the sun would make that for ever impossible. They are intended merely to conquer space, as is expressed by a frequent name for them, 'transits.' Or they are called 'cabin-boats.'

O those cabins! My noble friend, the Diwan of Mysore, to whom this journey is chiefly due, had warned me that I would not be able to stand up in the cabin. The next man to whom I mentioned this said that doubtless Mr. Madhava Rao, with his turban on, would not be able to stand up in most cabins; but that lesser men might manage it. When Diwan of Travancore, he had had built a special cabin-boat, of much more than the usual height, which I have heard of but have not seen.

My boat had on each side six oars, with a round disk at the end. That made twelve oars or rowers; but the relays consisted of sixteen men each. I did not discover what the extra four men did, unless it were to relieve the others in turn. The relays, paid by the Tehsildars, were said to be changed every 10 miles. The very sensible plan was to do the 130 miles or so to Trivandrum in three nights, stopping over in wayside bungalows during the day.

I have had two of these nights, but am lingering at Quilon. For two evenings I have sat in solitary grandeur on the bench on the top of the cabin, ascended to by a removable flight of steps. This point of vantage is glorious by night, but would be obviously impossible in the sun. I have watched the twelve rowers, facing me, bend with fair lustiness to their oars, making the foam and the boat fly. Their position was not wholly unlike that of the Athenian citizens, sitting, as they so hated to do, sore and breakfastless, on the leather pads of their galleys. It resembled this much more than the position of galley slaves, whose life, throughout the ages, has been reconstructed with such visionary force by Kipling.

A cook, for whom, with the lavish hospitality ashore, there was not much need, accompanied the cabin-boat. Once I saw him slip from the upper deck, where he sat at my feet, walk along the narrow plank between the two lines of rowers, and kick vigorously at a rower whose oar had ceased to act. It was a faint image of what the supervision of the slaves must once have been. For the rest, I often saw a man rest at his oar, while he prepared and swallowed some betel nut. The rowers really covered space, going at a steady rate of over four miles an hour. This is different from the Kashmir pace of a mile or two an hour, by means of lazy poling or towing.

Warned by some articles on 'Travancore Boat Songs,' by Mr. A. P. Smith, the Forest Officer and journalist, I set the rowers singing early, so that they might work it off before I wanted to sleep. It was a strange, unearthly clangour, not offensive, perhaps even attractive from force of habit, but far unlike the melodious singing on the water in Kashmir. For the rest, the boat, rushing in silence through the moonlight or the starlight, brought up the fascinating lines of Mortimer Collins:

> 'The oars of Ithaca dip so
>   Silently into the sea.
> That they wake not sad Calypso,
>   And the hero wanders free.'

The cabin portion occupied about one-half the boat. Yet the cabin was but three and a half feet high at the centre, less than that at the sides. It was not nice moving about bent double, or else on one's knees, or watching Bob Antony doing the latter. But there was a unique pleasantness in lying stretched out, with the doors shut and the Venetian shutters open, in the breeze created by the motion of the boat. I have had two such nights; and may perhaps have four more in all.

On the first morning we passed through Alleppey rather early, without my being aware of it. But later I was taking observations. So this is the famous lagoon life of Travancore! Palms, and palms, and palms! The whole effect is far cleaner than on Lake Wular in Kashmir. There is less mud, with fewer smells. This is due to the purifying breath and touch of the great salt sea. The average depth, here said to be ten or twelve feet, is at least twice that of Wular. The people lead an amphibious life. 'Every house is an island,' as a Tehsildar told me. No Europeans live in this watery section: they would not have the patience to get along, without roads. The people of North Travancore are rich by reason of their palms and their rice-fields, and also reputed to be idle. They are fat; manifestly not black, but brown; leading merry lives with their various kinds of boats, in which, unlike the Kashmiris, they often employ sails. What can we ever know about them? 'Little of this great world can I tell.'

At about 11 a.m. we reached Karumadi, 12 miles beyond Alleppey. Here an official from that station was awaiting me, with a whole staff of servants. There in the wilderness a table was several times set before me, on a certain handsome scale of hospitality. The house is unusually good for a Travellers' Bungalow. But it is not quite for all. A list is posted up of persons permitted to use it. In the afternoon the local Tehsildar called; a Brahman, although thirty-one, with a singularly candid, childlike face. In the twilight I tried to take a walk with the minor official — an intelligent man, but an F.M., Failed Matriculate. It was impossible to get about that drowned land, with water across the road every few hundred feet.

Chapter Seven - Quiet Days at Quilon

WALKING home with me one night last week, Bob Antony ventured the inquiry whether I belonged to the Military (evidently preferred) or the Civil Service. 'Neither!' There followed a moment of obvious cogitation, with this result: 'Himself: independent Master.' In vain I quoted Byron's 'Lord of himself, that heritage of woe.' Then Antony went on to say that at Trichur he had been much pressed for information on the above alternative, not only by peons, but by little boys in the street. He had thought it safest to stick to the story (I thank him for the age implied!) that I was a Colonel Sahib on 1500 rupees a month! Well, it makes me feel like an 'independent Master,' if not like a Colonel, to be treated so handsomely as I am by the Travancore State.

The only drawback here, and that is much, is the sapping climate. It would make me permanently tired. It is not a burning, brazen, or very obvious heat. But get round a corner, get for an instant out of the pleasant breeze that is generally moving, and you are at once crushed, annihilated. It has been said of Simla that men, or at least Englishmen, were not made to live 8000 feet above the sea. No more were they made to live within eight degrees of the equator. This peculiar heat seems to necessitate (as will appear when I speak of the Quilon Residency) a degree of luxury not required in other and less beautiful parts of India.

My readers may have noticed how, in these chapters, I never quite catch up with the subject promised in the title. Let me, so far as Malabar Head will allow, try here to pack various small miscellanies into one portmanteau paragraph. The young Jewesses of Cochin are believed to be sometimes very pretty. Heaven knows the children are; but I did not meet any older ones. The Jewish girls are said to be without exception virtuous and dirty. Continuing the last point, by all accounts the very dirtiest people in Travancore, as the most ignorant and contemned, are the Mahomedans. Here they have never borne rule: what excuse for existence have they? Next dirtiest to them, I hear, are the Christians; and among these, the Roman Catholic Syrians. At Cochin, so tropical it is, it was hard to realise that near 200 miles of sweeping coastland, or three degrees of latitude, yet lay before me to the Cape. A friend tells me, by the way, referring to the general title of these chapters, that Malabar, strictly speaking, ends a little beyond Cochin, including barely the northern fringe of Travancore. In popular parlance the name is certainly continued almost, or quite, to the Cape. And now I must spare a few sentences for a subject which means nothing to me, though it seems to be genuinely important. This is Rubber. Spell it with a capital, with many capitals, to represent its importance in the two States. There is said to be Money in Rubber. Here is an opening for capital; but the local men may like to keep a good thing to themselves. I have never, to my knowledge, seen a Rubber tree. Other things being equal, an industry ought to be encouraged which may help to cut out the accursed Congo product. At Trichur I met several prosperous rubber planters. I might have had invitations to their domains, but the journey of 20 miles and more into the lower hills was not for me. It takes about £100 to plant a single acre with Rubber, which will return 10 per cent clear. A single estate, managed by a young man, may cover 500 acres.

The famous open lagoons of Travancore extend for barely 100 miles, between Cochin and Quilon. From Quilon to Trivandrum there is still water communication for another 40 miles or so. But this is along narrow artificial canals, very different, as I am warned to expect from the mosquitoes tonight. I cannot realise that I have seen nearly all that I shall see of the lagoon life which so long haunted my imagination:

> 'Where the earlier ages sleep
> By hot lagoons of Malabar.'

A few glimpses, a few pictures: elusive unspeakably. How ignorant we all are, especially myself! For one thing, I saw nothing approaching that magical combination of something like Norwegian fiords and tropical jungle which Colonel Holdich seems to indicate. The mountains here do not reach the sea. Or, if this anywhere happens, it must be in places very hard for the European to come to, and almost impossible to photograph.

Scottish names beneath an almost equatorial sun! That suggests the transposed Simoïs and Scamander of the Trojan exiles! Just around the beautiful point facing the Residency is a Loch Lomond which I may see this evening. And the entrancing stretch of backwater between the Residency and that wooded foreshore is known, with some reason, as Loch Katrine. Just as in the Pacific islands, these false shores make a great part in the beauty of this coast. The most imposing spectacle is the view of the Quilon Residency from the water. It is bigger than the Trichur Residency, though it has not the advantage of being a home.

I have been here three nights and four days. No Collector in the Bombay Presidency has such quarters. Truly Government House at Mahableshwar is on a lesser scale — which may not be saying much! Such architecture seems to be found only in the Far South, and for the obvious reason that there alone is it necessary to the survival pf the white man.

This stately pile was reared some sixty years ago by the well-remembered Resident, General Cullen, who seems to have been a real mediaeval Lord, with some of the 'droits du seigneur.' The Maharaja's white palace, nearly opposite, is a lesser structure, though it tells in the green landscape, with the white obelisk before it. Two other bungalows are joined, by a curved covered way, symmetrically to the main Residency building. And from the end of one of these, to one of the opposite ends, is a Sabbath day's journey. The Trivandrum Residency is said to be even larger than this, but with no such grounds. These are not to be called by the familiar name of 'compound.' They are flanked on one side by the glorious backwater, and are estimated at 75 acres.

A corner of the grounds here incidentally includes a deer park, with some hundred deer, which is not exactly what one thinks of so near the equator. I have not yet seen them, as they are only visible at the twilight hour. Palm trees predominate less in the immediate landscape; there are mangoes, jackfruit, and other trees of some body. At most hours there is a delicious breeze through the upper floor of the Quilon Residency. When this is from the West and the water, as usual, it is all right. But old inhabitants dread the uncanny East wind, which the world over, as Du Maurier says, blows no man any good. In the hot season, which is deliberately stated to be already approaching at the end of December, I am told that when writing in this dry East wind, you can watch the corners of your paper curl up viciously. An illustration of the material basis of life is this, that good slumber can be purchased for a charge, even in a Residency, of six annas (6d.) per night for punkah coolies.

The Political Officer for these States must formerly have been the most fortunate of his tribe — I have heard nine Residencies counted up. But latterly Cochin has taken over one, while Travancore State has taken over several for the lordly entertainment of its guests. At Quilon I missed, by one day, the clever new Diwan (Prime Minister), Mr. Rajagopalachariar, going to Madras for the Christmas holidays. I also heard that Mr. Carr, the Resident, is on the High Range for some weeks to come, so that I shall hardly see him.

On my first day here there arrived by train, stopping for a few hours, the newly appointed Assistant Resident. Mr. Burn is a young man of about twenty-six, shaped to administration as two years can shape only in the I.C.S. Until two days before he had been in charge of the Dindigul subdivision, with 3000 square miles and 900,000 inhabitants, of the vast Madura district. He admired the change of scenery here, a refreshment for the tired eye, from the dry, red desolation of the British Districts adjoining: the people also are so much more attractive here. Mr. Burn had to go on at hot noon, by a special boat which admitted of standing up in it, and with the British flag flying at the rear. On the same day I had two interesting visitors; but it is evident that I cannot finish with Quilon in this chapter.

Chapter Eight - Quilon to Trivandrum

OF my two visitors on the first day at Quilon, one was the local Tehsildar, an attentive, able man, with a mind of his own. I saw much of him during the following days, and learned a good deal from him. His pay of 150 rupees (£10) a month is, as he puts it, 'not enough for an honest man.'

The other visitor was the Diwan Peshkar of the Quilon Division, Mr. V. I. Kesava Pillai, a very senior officer of Travancore State. These Diwan Peshkars correspond to the Collectors in British Districts. There are now four of them in Travancore, only one in Cochin. The leading district is that of Quilon, with 2300 square miles, and a population of 1,250,000. It contains the whole of the railway, and includes eleven out of the thirty-one taluks in Travancore. Mr. Kesava Pillai, an intellectual and kindly man, is a Nair. In a century past there has only been one Nair Diwan in Travancore; and as a rule Brahmans from outside the State have been called in (this is a sore point) to fill the post.

I must run together the impressions of the four days at Quilon. A thriving, far-spread city of 15,000 people, well known now as the terminus of a railway which does not financially pay. I had heard several boasts as to Travancore being a larger, richer country than Cochin, which, for one thing, seldom has a State guest as owning no State guest-house. The common houses at Quilon look fairly neat, with compounds of their own. The standard of comfort and cleanliness here is probably higher than in the Maratha country, higher than in most parts of India.

But an undeniable clear, early impression of Travancore is this: the excessive, the spick-and-span coquettish neatness of the average houses at Trichur and Ernakulam is not found here. It may exist northward from those places; but it does not exist southward. On the Cochin mainland I quickly noted that such words as 'huts' or 'hovels' no longer had any application. But already in the lagoon country of North Travancore the houses of the fishing or other people were mere huts. Even in Quilon there are many dwellings to which the same name would be no insult. This is also true of big, hilly Trivandrum, whence I write. So Mr. Banerji is evidently correct in claiming that nowhere in India is there the same standard of neatness and of comfort as in his humming little State. How far neatness necessarily means prosperity, or vice versa, is a deeper question, into which I will not go.

I *went for* the Civil Surgeon of. British Cochin, pleasantly encountered again at Quilon and in Trivandrum, as to the eradication of elephantiasis in his little promontory. Cannot all the King's horses and all the King's men stamp out this ignoble horror? The answer was startlingly illustrative of the material basis of life, and of how very many things, if not most things, depend Upon money. Yes, elephantiasis might be completely stamped out. All that is needed is a guaranteed supply of pure drinking water, preferably from the sea, as at Aden. The installation would cost about a lakh (£6,666) for British Cochin, another lakh for vile Matanchery, in State territory. Two lakhs outright would do this great work, plus about 2000 rupees a month for running expenses. All this is wholly beyond local resources. And neither Madras Presidency nor Cochin State is likely to see the glory of conquering elephantiasis as the Americans conquered yellow fever at Panama and in Cuba.

This Civil Surgeon offers yet a new type, for me, in the infinite complexity of Indian life. He belongs to the community, numbering perhaps 4000, of

Kashmiri Brahmans long settled in Northern India. He is not a Brahmo, because he has no need to be. He is the second highly superior Kashmiri that I have known, the other being his schoolmate, the Diwan Daya Kishan.

Quilon boasts a scanty, not to say paltry, beach, where the better classes gather of an evening. Just here, and beyond to the lighthouse, a fine harbour might be made. I am told, not only by natives, that this is prevented by British jealousy, chiefly represented by some Madras merchants. It is said that a great port in a Native State would not be tolerated. There are about a dozen Europeans, whose chief excuse for a sweltering existence is business. People dress mercifully little in Malabar; yet at Quilon there are often dinners where dressing is required. The Darragh Cotton Mills, with all their clangour of machinery, are worth a visit. Here are 650 men; and more interesting, 150 women — or rather young girls, up to marriage.

I had thought of going laterally across Travancore from west to east, by taking the railway journey inland as far as Shenkota on the State frontier, through 60 miles of so-called unrivalled Ghat scenery. But the trip did not come off. I was not sorry to have a quiet Christmas. Two Christians, even of the most nominal type, like to forgather on that day. I collected a new opinion, namely, that morally Malabar is the sink of India. This is but the quoted opinion of one man; and is not meant as a sweeping criticism of Malabar morals. It chiefly refers, not to sexual matters, but to the alleged persistent underhanded and intriguing habits of the people. I used to wonder, since I was sometimes prostrated by the heat even in the mighty Residency, what would be my condition in one of the low-roofed bungalows outside. Probably the condition of a corpse.

From Quilon to Trivandrum I brought down a pleasant-faced young man, with acquaintances in common with myself, and of a wandering life. He turned out to be a son of the only Nair Diwan of Travanoore, some thirty years before. The Malabar anomaly must here be remembered, that the son of a Diwan is a lees important personage than his nephew. My new friend told me, among other things, one which I have confirmed in Trivandrum, and which (but I am very ignorant) may well justify the worst opinion of this coast, it seems that a man is not allowed to talk freely with, or freely to approach, his younger sister, after she has grown up. Incredible as it may seem, a brother and sister in an enlightened family, by driving out together, have given occasion to bad talk; The next step, logically, would be to import suspicion into the relations between father and daughter; and this step has been taken. I will not pursue the gruesome subject. What a poisoning of the springs of family life!

The alleged careless morality of Malabar is something not apparent on the surface, something reversed and intangible. Real carelessness might well be better than such thought-taking!

A cabin-boat becomes more comfortable when one is put up to certain things. The crews, mostly Christians, were at their worst so near to Christmas. They took some thirteen hours for the 40 miles. In the tree tops were still hanging pretty Christmas lanterns. We went by many narrow ways, where the oars hardly had room to work. We passed in the dark a place I should much have liked to see, Anjengo (British territory), now a lonely shooting place for snipe. Here was brought up, a long century and a half ago, in an isolation we can hardly grasp, Sterne's 'Eliza,' whose story is well told in James Douglas's 'Bombay and Western India.' Anjengo was also the birthplace of Robert Orme, no longer compared to Thucydides, yet still dear to Colonel Newcome, and to a few other Anglo-Indians. We passed through several tunnels, one of them a mighty work, where an open blind was knocked off the cabin-boat. The same voyage, by 'wollam' or open canoe, costs, I have just learned, 3 ½ rupees.

Shall I ever catch up with myself in these Malabar letters? The very climate makes one feel like the man who was born half an hour late, and who never, through life, could make up that half-hour. I cannot begin to tell here of Trivandrum, where, for several days, every kindness has been shown me. I found a handsome letter from the Diwan, in Madras, hoping that Travancore was interesting me. Was it not! He committed me to the care of his substitute here, the genial Chief Secretary to the Government.

Chapter Nine - Trivandrum— The Maharaja

'The Protected State of Cocoanutcore!
Where dwells a worthy and well-oiled nation,
Blest with a faultless administration;
The brightest land, with the lightest tax,
And an annual surplus of fifty lacs;
Where happy ryots ne'er pestered by famines.
Till fields, in subjection to blessed Brahmins.
A land of peace, a land of delight,
Where every one, everywhere, always does right.
Where white men, living in meek minority,
Acknowledge Brahminical superiority.
In short, and Pm sure I cannot say more,
'Tis a heaven upon earth, this Cocoanutcore.'

Chutney Lyrics.
'The Good Sir Gammon Row.'

THE above verses are not my own. I wish they were, though quoted verse is paid for, and original not I Who, in this generation, knows 'The Chutney Lyrics'? It is a neat little volume, published by Higginbotham, in Madras, way back in 1871. As for the neatness of the verse, that is unmistakable. There is both comic and literary force. Two copies existed in Trivandrum, the property of the same book-loving administrator. The last preceding State guest here, Mr. R. C. Dutt, carried off one of the copies last October. With all

44

his reading, it was a revelation to him. 'Oh, give me that book!' he cried. If Mr. Dutt did not know 'Chutney Lyrics,' others may be excused to whom it is but the echo of a name, or less.

Who wrote this book of rare promise? A young man, I am told, named Caldwell, the son of a missionary Bishop of Tinnevelly. He died soon after, I believe in Travancore. Doubtless more could be learned about this earlier, incomplete Kipling. Caldwell's very name for this State, Cocoanutcore — how awfully good it is! That is Kerala, the coastal territory beginning where Malabar proper is said to end, in the North of Travancore. It is alleged to differ in several respects from Malabar, and to allow much less freedom to its women.

The very word Kerala means palm. And to show how the word and the thought predominate here, as I write comes in a note from the scholarly kinsman of the ruling family, whom I am to meet this afternoon — the Maharaja's cousin and brother-in-law, as he is called, Kerala Varma.

The poem of Caldwell's, quoted from above, 'The Good Sir Gammon Row,' is a very strong attack upon a very strong man, on whose traces I come at every step, the late Raja Sir T. Madhava Rao. Of course, Brahmanical superiority has greatly diminished in Travancore during the last forty years, in common with priestcraft the world over. The last lines of the rather long poem are:

> 'All truth, all justice is fudge
> When a Brahmin is judged by a Brahmin Judge!'

A descendant of Sir Gammon Row has the candour to admit to me that this is still essentially true in Travancore.

During four days already at Trivandrum I have come into closer touch with many of the people, things, and types of Malabar, or perhaps Kerala. I found awaiting me a promised letter from Professor Macdonell, giving interesting details about the condition of Sanskrit learning in these parts. In Cochin State there are said to be, for example, 4000 Brahmans who can repeat the whole of one of the Vedas.

I am lodged at the Trivandrum Travellers' Bungalow, which is the most convenient place in every respect. Even normally, it is superior to the ordinary building of the sort. But it may be quite transformed with two rooms reserved, with special furniture and servants, with flowers and books, and with a carriage always waiting unharnessed in the shade. Best of all the additions is a punkah, worked day and night by unusually faithful imps. Without this punkah I might not have survived, and certainly could not have written the last two chapters. Beneath it deep slumber may be had, from which, however, one may wake up languid. That is the climate. But how different from the frequent Bombay condition of tossing sleepless for two nights, and then sleeping from mere exhaustion on the third night!

Trivandrum is a city of some 60,000 people, manifestly a capital. It is seated on many hills or hillocks, with trying hollows in between. Cyclists here have to give up cycling as a bad job. The public carriages, spacious and comfortable, cannot keep up an average of more than five miles an hour. What with the ups and downs, the reddish roads, and the greenery around (but this is composed of palms), there is more than a suggestion of Mahableshwar. Trivandrum is but eight degrees from the equator. In that latitude every fraction counts — like a quarter of an inch at the end of a man's nose. This is about the sultriest place, during the day, that I have ever been in. But it rapidly cools off with the evening. A Civil Surgeon was not long in seeing that this is due to the sandy soil, which quickly absorbs and quickly releases the sun's heat.

My immediate host and entertainer has been A. J. Vieyra, for the last six years Chief Secretary to the Travancore Government. In the Diwan's temporary absence, Mr. Vieyra seems to make most of the wheels go, much like a permanent Undersecretary of State at home. He is a jovial giant of fifty, standing 6 feet 1 inch, able to work, even in this climate, twelve or fourteen hours a day. In hours yet further stolen from sleep, Mr. Vieyra is also a man of letters — a man of European culture, who has never seen Europe. He is a raconteur, and can cap a quotation with any one. 'What does Shakespeare say of a given situation?' — and the right passage comes out! The Chief Secretary is of recent Portuguese, and also Dutch, stock, unconnected with Goa.

Local 'institutions' are apt to be dull dogs; and I was not sorry to find most of them closed. But it was a restful delight to wander through the shady Trivandrum Library, which is on a scale far beyond what could be expected; and to hear of Mr. Dutt's keenness on books: 'Here's a new edition' — 'That's rubbish!'

Of his Maharaja, Mr. Vieyra says: 'So far as I can learn, there is no other ruler in India like him — so intelligent, so patient, so devoted to the good of his subjects.' I had also been told that the ruler knew more about his own country than any of his officers did.

I was summoned to meet H.H. at 6.46 a.m. yesterday. The hour is not so dreadful as it seems, since Trivandrum time is half an hour behind the ordinary. Yet it did remind me of an awful scramble I had in London, long ago, to get to the breakfast of an Indian pro-consul, from miles away, at 'quarter past eight' of a December morning, arriving half an hour late, after all. That would not do with the Maharaja of Travancore, who is the most punctual of rulers.

There was a freshness and delight about Trivandrum streets at sunrise, but all this has to be paid for in weariness later. At the Palace within the Fort there were few guards. Before a wall adorned with curious frescoes of elephants and of dragons, stood two purple peons. Within a plain hall, flush with the steps, stood the Maharaja.

I could write an article about him and about the interview of some forty minutes. But it seems better to write only a paragraph, for which express permission was given. The Maharaja perfectly remembered the visit of 'Mr. Loti' eight years before. It seems that Loti could understand English when addressed, but could not speak it. He was accompanied by Mr. Mackenzie, the Resident, who translated for him, and who afterwards Englished his account of Travancore for the Maharaja. (This forms a neat pamphlet of about forty compact pages.) Such facts make Loti's attitude towards the English seem stranger than ever. It may be remembered how inscrutable and alien Loti had found the Maharaja; I found the same ruler quiet, even hushed, in manner, and of great courtesy. But I prefer not to discuss my kind host. So the year, which began for me in Kashmir ends in Kerala. I hope this week to have a drive to Comorin.

Chapter Ten - The Little Ranis and Their Guardian

THE very pleasantest hour which I have had in Malabar was perhaps the one which I was allowed to spend with the little Ranis (Queens) of Travancore. The position of these still wee Princesses is one to touch the imagination. There is nothing quite like it in the world, though it suggests the position of the Queen of Holland when a child. Chinese documents of a dozen odd centuries ago, quoted in Dr. Stein's 'Ancient Khotan,' speak of a Kingdom of Women, 'Strirajya,' 3000 'li' to the south of Khotan. A 'li' is about the fifth part of a mile, which would make the distance but 600 miles. I leave it to the learned to say whether this allusion can possibly be due to any echo of the strange matriarchal institutions of Malabar.

The Sanskrit Chronicle of Kashmir, by the way, places its Kingdom of Women, whose warriors could vanquish their enemies merely by baring their disquietingly lovely bosoms, amid the inhospitable wastes due north. I am also told that Malabar is constantly spoken of as 'Stri-Malabar,' with reference to the peculiarly strong position of women here. The important legal question here still is, not what man's son is any one, but what woman's son is he.

I do not want to make a disquisition when I should be describing two delicious children; yet it is important to place them. The present Maharaja, aged fifty, is the last survivor by blood of a fine which was adopted into the ruling House more than a century ago. Adoption plays as great a part in Indian life as it did in the fife of ancient Rome; and, as in Rome, it is held to take the place of blood-relationship in the fullest degree. Adoption has been so much in the air here latterly that one is apt to think of it as more frequent than it really is. The Travancore dynasty is believed to be mentioned in the Mahabharata, and in any case is ancient enough. Yet before these little Ranis, there had been but six royal adoptions during as many centuries.

It is the result of the matriarchal system of succession that a man's, and especially a ruler's, son is unimportant as compared to his sister's son. A Maharaja's son can never succeed. He is called a Tambi; and there is an entire caste or sept of Tambis. I have seen, standing unnoticed in a shop, the son of the highly accomplished late Maharaja. The present ruler also has lawful progeny, which does not count. Rather topsy-turvy, isn't it? And his line would have died out but for the adoptions of 1900. Not to go into family details, there are normally two outstanding Princesses, called Ranis, the son of one of whom should be the next Maharaja. They may be the sisters, the nieces, or, as was lately the case, the female cousins (adopted sisters), of the Maharaja. These Ranis are royal, but their husbands are not.

Classic words for caste are used in Malabar which are no longer heard in many parts of India. The word Sudra is constantly used to designate Nairs and other quite swagger people. And the warlike sound of Kshattriya seems to mean a very limited, persistent, and endogamous clan, which includes the ruling family. Fair! It has been a constant wonder to me how fair many people are in this romantic uttermost end of India, which ought to be negritic, but which is not, or which has ceased to be so.

Never was there such a delusion as mine in imagining that I was coming into a country of black people. These exist just across the Ghats, a little to the eastwards: I am told, without much grasping it, that the moist sea air whitens, and also beautifies, the people who were once essentially Tamils. Be it that, or the alleged pervading Brahman blood, the people I see are mostly amazingly fair, as well as good-looking. I would not hesitate to say that they average fairer than in the Maratha country, 600 miles further north. Fascinating problems of colour and of race! But no people in these parts, unless for some Brahmans, can be fairer than the small Kshattriya stock, from which the Ranis come.

As a rule the husbands (people are careful to say 'consorts') to the Ranis do not count. But there has been an exception in the case of the consort of H.H. Lakshmi Bayi, C.I., the late Senior Rani. This lady was greatly beloved and admired. She was childless; and she died in 1902. She had been specially decorated by Queen Victoria for her constancy in refusing to put away her husband at a time, more than thirty years ago, when strong pressure was brought upon her for this purpose, when he was exiled and under the displeasure of the then Maharaja. He is now the guardian of the little Ranis, Kerala Varma, C.S.I., also called Valia Koil Tampuran. He is an author in the vernacular, and in Sanskrit. In particular, his poem on his exile and his wife's constancy, called 'The Peacock Messenger,' seems to hold a unique place in the small Malayalam literature. He is easily the first citizen of the State, apart from the Diwans who come and go. By birth, Kerala Varma is a younger brother of the aged feudatory Raja of Parapanad. He is now about sixty-two. He is a nobleman, a scholar, also, alas! with all his gentleness, a devotee — but not a 'Highness.' But he will pardon my not speaking of him here save in his capacity of guardian to his very charming charges, who are by blood his dead wife's great-nieces.

From eight to a dozen and more years ago, the question of adoption was a burning one. The ruling House then seemed in danger of extinction. It has since become extinct, save for the Maharaja. The late Senior Rani, cousin of the Maharaja, was tactfully urged, especially by the late Sir Sheshia Shastri, to make an adoption which would supply the State with children who would be as if her own. The children were at hand, in the two tiny daughters of her two nieces. They were born in the month of November, one in 1895, and the other in 1896. I have heard these fine children called 'picked specimens' of the Kshattriya race, and so they are. But the late Senior Rani did not have to wander far to find them. These are the little Ranis, Setu Lakshmi Bayi, Senior Rani, and Setu Parvati Bayi, Junior Rani. The rest of the names seems to be traditional; but the 'Setu' is something particular. There was, before their births (as before the birth of the little Tsarevitch), a pilgrimage to Rameshvaram, with performance of the 'Seta Snanam' expiatory rites — Whence the epithetic double name.

These little ladies were adopted into the royal family, with national ceremonies, in Angast, 1900. They both became Junior Ranis, granddaughters of the then Senior Bani, and thus also of Kerala Varma, and adopted great, or grand-nieces of the Maharaja. On the death of the late Senior Rani, some two years later, little Seta Lakshmi became Senior Rani, and Seta Parvati the only Junior Bani. Each of them is 'Her Highness,' and is stated to be very conscious of the fact. Their governess says that sometimes she can only appeal, with them, to the 'Noblesse oblige'; but that the appeal always tells.

Upon these little girls, though (me hardly likes to think of it in that light, depends the succession to the throne of Travancore. From one of them must be born the next Maharaja. It was thought that, in order to be legal, their nominal marriages must take place before they reached the age of twelve. There were therefore the recent wedding ceremonies, which, many will remember. I will not stop to speak of the youthful Kshattriya husbands. The Senior Bani's husband is still quite a youth. The Junior Bani's husband is some half-dozen years older than the other, and is, by great exception, a gradual of Madras University.

'Their Highnesses are coming,' said the kind and venerable Kerala Varma. Down the vista of the long hall advanced, with conscious dignity, two of the daintiest little figures imaginable. I had not been prepared for the arrangement of the hair, which was done, according to a national custom, in an enormous wing over each little forehead. There was I know not what Burmese or Japanese effect about this, suggesting that slight Mongolian touch which is undeniable along this coast. The Ranis had on large tight-fitting silk jackets, one of crimson, one of green. They also wore, bunched up in pleats high over the stomach, some snowy drapery, not at all to be called by the familiar Indian name of 'sari.' There was also some gold, with sparkling gems. The children were several sizes smaller than I would have thought from their pictures, and from what I had heard. They are now (January, 1908) little more than turned twelve and eleven years of age respectively. The Senior Rani stands three inches higher than the Junior: so little Setu Parvati Bayi has her work cut out for the next year! I was told that Nair women (yet these are not at all Nair) are built somewhat small.

They are both of them little beauties; and as fair as some Europeans. The elder is more reserved, more conscious of her dignity, and also (I hope I am giving away no secret!) the quicker pupil. They are, indeed, a lovely pair. I could not wonder at Kerala Varma saying that since the death of his consort the care and the companionship of these children have made the greatest delight in his life. have been adopted as two sisters. But by blood they are first cousins. Their mothers are sisters. One of these is always in residence at the Palace, by turns, and both the girls call her 'mother.' With each mother comes (to illustrate the subordinate position of the mere male in Malabar) her husband, the father of one of the girls. It was a happy home life that was indicated.

When the little Ranis entered, the hall was still somewhat dim. It was hardly 7 a.m. This is the hour when Europeans generally have to meet members of the ruling family. The reason for this is one which provoked Lord Roberts, who had known nothing like it in any other part of India, to a possibly uncharitable remark in his 'Forty-one Years.' Malabar is blessedly free from any imitation of that wicked invention of Mahomed, the purdah. There is only one woman in Travancore who is at all 'gosha' (condemned to seclusion), as they say. This is the consort of H. H. the Maharaja, herself not royal. And she is not really 'gosha,' since she' latterly goes out driving in a carriage with blinds half raised, and has let her portrait appear.

But religion takes it out, in Malabar, by an exaggerated development of Touch-not-ism. Europeans must visit royalty thus early because their touch pollutes, because the purifying bath is taken at 8 a.m., and only after that can food be tasted. One hesitates to recall such facts in the midst of courtesy so great as that I have received.

After about a quarter of an hour, came in the charming young governess of the Ranis, Miss Watts. She helped the conversation to flow, though the ice had already been broken. The Ranis speak quite firm good English, having been at it for at least six years. They also study in Malayalam and in Sanskrit. In the last language they do not try to speak, but read easy stories. I inquired about their dolls. The Senior has five dolls, and the Junior, as is but right, seven. Two magnificent dolls were given by Lady Ampthill. The Ranis are just starting a stamp album. I heard all about their little lives; how, in addition to a deal of pious ceremonial, they go out driving in the afternoon, or play badminton with their consorts and others. They are evidently strong and healthy. It was pretty to watch their drawing-books, and others, marked 'Sr' and 'Jr' respectively. I saw them playing on big vinas, seated on the floor. I also heard them, in the schoolroom, playing the piano with a good touch.

It is so often said that Indian girls have no childhood. But these evidently have a good childhood. It is to be hoped that, with the help, of Watts, this may be continued for some time yet.

Chapter Eleven – 'This Last Corner'

THE ten chapters preceding were all written literally from Malabar, and as nearly as possible on the spot. But what with the Malabar Head, the insidious oppression of the climate, with limited time and strength, it was impossible to keep up with these or any other letters during the rush of departure from the country. Yet, as a friend chaffingly told me, I had not been in such haste as to tumble over myself. I was in the two Malabar States for a month and some days — or about twice as long as Loti ever was. How he took his notes, mental or other, seems to be one of the mysteries of genius.

Loti, though this is not apparent in his narrative, stopped at the Residency in Trivandrum, and was officially conducted almost everywhere. The Koil Tampuran (Kerala Varnia, C.S.I.) showed me a small framed photograph of him, already faded, which Loti gave him eight years ago. The author appears as a smart naval officer, his breast so bedizened with decorations that one wonders where they can all have come from.

Readers may remember his complaint, at the end of the fascinating Malabar portion, that he had been passed through the country (I quote from memory) as if in a sort of magic barque, with the utmost courtesy, but as rapidly as possible, and having been allowed to see as little as possible of the inner meaning of things. I used to inquire in advance if that would be my experience. No, I was cordially told, times had changed even in these few years. But I heard in Trivandrum that Loti's complaint was possibly justified. And if anything prevented his seeing things, it would have been not native secretiveness, but the ineradicable English official jealousy of a foreigner in a Native State. Even so far from the Frontier as here — even in this Last Corner!

So the two or three letters from Malabar, necessary to complete the subject, are written from the nearest halting-place outside, while still everything is fresh in my mind. The order was but for ten letters. But to keep within the four corners of such editorial estimates is notoriously hard. Thus, Professor Macdonell was ordered to get his abstract of Sanskrit Literature, in the forthcoming Historical volume of the Imperial Indian Gazetteer, into forty pages. But the subject was too much for him; and he confesses to sixty!

My articles written in Malabar, with an exception or two, had the advantage of being corrected, as to matters of fact, by the best authority accessible upon the spot, whether Tehsildar, Diwan, or another. Such chapters can only be superficial, impressionistic. According to a high authority, you must travel up and down Travancore, for at least six months, at great expense of strength and money, before you can begin to consider that you know it. With all my respect for the exact fact, I fear that blunders, for which I still invite correction, may have crept into the preceding chapters. Such are still more likely in the remaining chapters. But at least there will have been no wilful mistakes.

'This Last Corner.' The phrase came from a clever young Head Clerk, with a Maratha name, a grandson of the great Sir T. Madhava Rao, who had been told off to attend me in Trivandrum. This brings up the predominance of the Maratha Brahmans, and especially of one clan, in the States through which I have been travelling. There can be no greater compliment to your Marathi than to say that you speak like a Rao. In Mysore the First Councillor of State is Raja Madhava Rao's only surviving child, Mr. Ananda Rao. To his kindly courtesy I owed two useful letters of introduction in Travancore. One was to his brother-in-law, Mr. Padmanabha Rao, of Quilon, himself the son of a notable Diwan of some twenty years ago, named Ram Rao. This gentleman suggests the high-bred, athletic type of an English squire, but with the limitation that orthodoxy forbids him to be a sportsman. This limitation is unknown to many of the Brahmans of the North, as witness the Diwan of Kashmir. In Travancore I soon ceased to count the sons and nephews of ex-Diwans whom I met.

The one public monument in Trivandrum is the statue, too short, yet impressive, of Raja Sir T. Madhava Rao — 'the good Sir Gammon Row.' In a house close beside it, I can hardly say below it, lives his grandson, my friend and guide, who has also numerous kinsmen. In his earliest years he was confidential Private Secretary to his grandfather, who died in 1891, barely turned sixty-three. A delightful paragraph might be made up, if this were quite the place for it, from his memories of the veteran Diwan's acts and words. The old man was a High Tory. He distrusted, perhaps with good reason, some modern tendencies, such as the mania for English education. He would have liked to see primogeniture grafted upon the Indian joint-family system; and to perpetuate his title of Raja. He died a millionaire, in rupees (£66,666), after having lived upon a scale which few Indians, not sovereigns, have attempted.

Abundant and unique materials exist, chiefly in the hands of Mr. Ananda Rao, of Bangalore, for a Life and Letters of Sir Madhava Rao such as has been written of few Indians. It would be a book of international importance, helping to reveal Indians to Europe at large. But it should not be delayed until the world has ceased to be interested even in this mighty administrator of three States (Travancore, Indore, Baroda), whom his namesake of Mysore, for example, believes to have been the greatest Indian of the century.

Cape Comorin I had to give up. This is the only one of the great Capes of the world which orthodox Hindus can visit. There, on the evening of the full moon, you may watch the sun sinking in the sea on the one hand, while the moon rises from the sea on the other. I was within 50 miles of the Cape, or less than one degree. But, so near to the equator, they were insuperable miles to me. There was talk of sending me in one of the few motors. But something was the matter, as something generally is, with the chauffeur. Time was lacking; nor could I otherwise face the bullock-cart method. So

Comorin, the Cape of the Virgin, at the mingling of three seas, remains for the present unvisited.

A visit to the Museum is well worthwhile, if only because of the five big canvases by the late Raja Ravi Varma. Some of these I knew from engravings; but the rich colouring of the originals adds enormously to the effect. Ravi Varma's drawing is said to leave something to desire. But he has colour, and, what is more, atmosphere. His Sitas and his Draupadis! There is here a noble ideal of Indian womanliood. I am told that, technically (as in the greater length of the arms), it is modelled on the womanhood of Northern India, where, of course, the epics belong.

But in this last, for so long this last, corner of India, there is a frequent female type of which any country might be proud. My sight of the little Ranis had revealed to me what I was losing by leaving Trivandrum before the many Girls' Schools had reopened. These must be perfect gardens of beauty. Loti visited but one, of which he has left quite a luscious description. The ivory fairness of these women and girls is a perpetual wonder. I do not wish to hurt any feelings; and the Nairs are getting sensitive about their supposed Brahman blood. But a high authority said to me: 'They get their brains, their complexions, everything, from the Brahmans.'

I had been told in Bangalore that I would find Trivandrum an even more intellectual city. I would not believe it. Yet so it seems to be. But the ability seems to lack direction, practicality, contact with the earth. It is an intellect in the void, so to speak. To a tantalising degree, most of the prominent people I met were not Malayalis at all. The real people of Travancore, the Nairs, have not produced a Diwan for some thirty years, since the father of the friend whom I brought down from Quilon. The reapers of the harvest are most generally Brahmans, and even these not usually those of the country, of whom so much is heard. The administrators are apt to be Maratha Brahmans, or else, like the new Diwan, Tamil Brahmans. There is one very prominent Telugu Brahman.

Chapter Twelve - Across Travancore

TRIVANDRUM, and in fact Cocoanutcore generally, would make a delightful Lotus Eaters' Land. It is a nice country in which to lie on one's back — on one's back, under the punkah, doing nothing, hardly thinking, but recovering from the last thought of exertion. For work the climate is not fitted. A public servant has stated that you may, with resolution, work four hours a day, but no more. That is not so bad as the case of a former Bishop of Bombay, who used to claim that he could not work more than two hours a day in the climate of Bombay city. The next stop is to divide the working hour up into fifteen-minute intervals. A country for the Labour Leader's famous principle: Never to work between meals!

Europeans are apt to think that they cannot survive at all in the Tropics without eating and sleeping very largely. But even in Trivandrum may be found successful advocates of the simple life. I have been surprised at the number of big Europeans, six-footers more or less, whom I have met in Malabar. Perhaps the others died in infancy. I cannot understand Indians living through such burning days upon their vegetable trash. But what a glorious thing it must be economically! A rich Indian can feed like a fighting-cock on 8 annas a day. How much more money must be worth to him than to us! That raises an economic question, into which I will not enter. I was once, in Trivandrum, taken up a ladder into a sort of loft, where I would snuff out quickly enough in the course of a summer's day. It was the 'studio' (as people will say for 'study') of a Professor drawing Rs. 320 (£21 odd) a month. I was told that he probably banked over three-quarters of his pay.

Work is the one thing not to be thought of in Trivandrum. But why work, with the cocoanut trees growing for you? The average cocoanut tree brings in 10 rupees a year; and there are few men in Cocoanutcore who do not own some. An estimate which I have already given, and which was passed by a high authority, namely, that two or three trees, with some fish from the backwater, will support an ordinary family through the year, appears to be exaggerated. But half a dozen trees will do so. In Travancore there are hardly any houseless men. The poorest has a share in an enclosed homestead. What an amazing, what a democratic and blessed fact!

In the twilight, and sometimes also at other hours of the day, you may drive abroad without too much exertion. The very horses in Trivandrum are languid. The climate, with the local hills, is said to wear out a horse in five years – specially the big Walers. There would seem to be some natural unfitness along this coast for many forms of animal life. The cattle and goats imported into Cochin degenerate into mere rats. It was therefore a constant wonder to me that the human race throve so well, producing such creditable specimens. The Diwan tells me that the more arid parts of Travancore, southwards from Trivandrum, produce, like Scotland, a stalwart race of men, soldiers six feet high and more.

As for the women, many of them are amazingly fair, in both senses of the word. How did they get into this last and languid comer of India? I call upon Sir Herbert Bisley to explain. Some of the Nair women are fairer than any women in fabled Kashmir, or in all the twenty-six degrees of latitude that stretch between.

For the rest, to one who has lived in Kashmir, there is much in Travancore, even in its unlikeness, to remind him of the Valley. 'The two best countries in India,' they have been called. At opposite extremities, they know nothing of each other. But there is a similar natural and superlative picturesqueness. Countries for artists to revel in. Things fall unsolicited into picture form — whether a bit of landscape, a little group, or a child in a doorway. Just such

54

visions do not abound in the Maratha country. Yet for a permanence I would prefer that.

The life of India has little, pitifully little, of the glorious open sea. It therefore counts for much, at Trivandrum, that there is something of a beach, upon the full ocean, which you may reach by a toilsome drive of three or four miles. On several evenings it was a real refreshment to wend thither, and to play for a little with the in-rolling breakers. But this beach, somehow, always made me think of Loti, rather than of the people of the country.

A very distinguished citizen of Travancore is the Senior and retiring Diwan Peshkar, Nagam Aiya, who has five times served as Acting Diwan. Mr. Nagam Aiya, still but fifty-seven and a fine figure of a man, is the oldest graduate of the Trivandrum College. I was introduced to him by his close friend, Mr. Ananda Rao, first Councillor of Mysore, who shares with him his literary tastes. (Both of these lettered administrators retired during 1908.) Mr. Nagam Aiya is the accepted literary man of the State. He has been settled in Travancore for generations past, yet is a Telugu Brahman, and, like so many other prominent men, not quite of the soil. As a young graduate, he began to attract the notice of the gifted previous Maharaja, not yet on the throne, by 1872 or earlier. He conducted the census of 1891.

But his great work is the 2000 pages of the 'State Manual.' These three volumes, or the thinnest of them, would be enough to knock a man down with. The 'State Manual' is the best, practically the only, repository of the latest information about Travancore. Mr. V. P. Madhava Rao, an old political opponent of the writer, who is severely glanced at in its pages, delights in it. He gave me his own copy, saying that there was, on the whole, no book like it.

But as I was complaining, at the beginning, of the lack of obvious books about Malabar, I may mention several outstanding ones. On reaching Trivandrum, I found one cubic foot of literature about the State awaiting me from the Government. Roughly corresponding in value to the 'State Manual' for Travancore (of which there was a second copy) is the valuable Volume I of the 'Census Report' for Cochin by Mr. Sankara Menon. There is also the 'Census Report,' well spoken of, for Travancore. A popular little book seems to be Mr. Panikkar's 'Malabar and its Folk.'

Mr. Nagam Aiya lives both in his 'Brahman village' (alas! not indigenous), through which I was most pleasantly and courteously shown, and on a noble, breezy estate of a hundred acres, a mile or two from Trivandrum, his 'Hill,' as he calls it, or Tirumallai Lodge. He seems to be a rich man; yet he is liable to have to feed forty or fifty kinsmen daily. That is the pleasant Indian system, so different from English snobbery. A man in the highest position will not disown a kinsman in the lowest. I have even known a native Prime Minister (Diwan) who was related to one of his own chauffeurs, and not ashamed of the fact.

Of humble position in Trivandrum are two writers who have done, and will do, good work. One is Mr. Ramanatha Aiya, a clerk in the public offices, whose name, again, shows him to be what in Travancore is called a 'foreigner.' He has produced a capital 'Brief Sketch of Travancore' of some 250 pages, besides numerous interesting monographs. The other is Mr. Kukuswami Aiyengar, the loyal Private Secretary to the Koil Tampuran, Kerala Varma.

I have long been accustomed to say that orthodoxy is everywhere unintelligent. Yet there seems to be a momentary exception when one meets Nagam Aiya and one or two others. Orthodoxy rages and holds high revel in Malabar. It is wilful. It is also expensive, as I remarked when hearing a great man denounced for eating on a railway train (which is forbidden for Hindus), and learned that it would take the speaker 500 rupees to journey to Madras, since he would have to be accompanied by half a dozen Brahman servants, besides stopping over several times. How can men of intellect, men who get out and read the best English books, stop to consider such paltriness? 'If fifty families of our standing — but there are not five such families — would join us in making a stand, something might be done.' So it is local opinion which rules. 'I would be pointed at, or worse, as I walked through the streets of my Brahman village!'

I noted in Mysore that South India, so far advanced intellectually and politically, without, for one thing, the shadow of any sedition, was strangely backward socially. This is still more notable in the maritime States. There seems not to be a Brahmo anywhere south of Trichur. The Baja of Cochin is said to be an enemy of 'Europe-returned' mmi. The Maharaja of Travancore, without going so far, watches the orthodoxy of his servants. A very bright boy of nineteen, who has a moral right to have a try for the Civil, cannot go to England because of a miserable superstition. He is one of many. What does it matter that the ancient Hindus voyaged bravely over the neighbouring seas? Local Southern opinion now forbids it!

How madly Hindu orthodoxy varies between North and South — yet in each quarter so cocksure that it alone is right! My Kashmiri secretary used to amuse me by declaring that the few Hindus of Kashmir, all of them Brahmans, were alone 'pukka' (genuine), all the Hindus of vast India being but 'kutcha' (make-believe). 'What sort of Brahmans are those?' I was asked in Trivandrum, when I said that Kashmir Brahmans could not get along for a day without animal food. Poisonous spirit of orthodoxy, of narrowness, of exclusion, everywhere the same! So I lately set Bob Antony, my faithful Roman Catholic servant, to disputing with a Syrian Christian clerk who had been sent to conduct us to a Forest Bungalow. Each other Church, it appeared, including the Protestant, was 'not good.'

I must record hero a highly suggestive thought which was thrown out in Trivandrum. What would have been the result had Englishmen, on first coming to India, adopted the ceremonial cleanliness of the Brahmans, kept only Brahman cooks, qualified themselves to eat with Brahmans, avoiding contact with sweepers and outcasts? Might not races and faiths have then come together in quite another, and a more friendly, combination? Perhaps Brahmanical exclusiveness would have defeated any effort at either commensal or marriage relations. But the thought is greatly worth considering.

I must also mention one respect in which the Maharaja of Travancore, protector of orthodoxy though he be, is more broadminded than some Indian rulers. He fed me daily with far better beef than can be had in most District Centres. Contrast this with the monstrous pretension of the Maharaja of Kashmir (whose gentler virtues I have also seen and recorded) to control the diet of visitors to his State.

While in Trivandrum I was allowed to examine some hundreds of manuscript letters written by the previous Maharaja of Travancore, known as Vishaham, from the constellation under which he was born. This is a subject upon which I wish to say here only a few sentences. This ruler, born in 1837, reached the throne in 1880, and died in 1885 after a brilliant reign of only five years. He was uncle to the present Maharaja, also uncle to the late consort of Kerala Varma. The late Maharaja Vishaham was in some respects a born man of letters. He was also a statesman of Curzonian stiffness and infallibility; also a devotee. Probably no Indian sovereign of the last century had such distinguished qualities. Perhaps 1000 of his letters, often very brief, could yet be collected and published. Such a volume, with some connecting biographical matter, would be a revelation to the world of what is possible in Hindu fife, comparable only to the desired Life and Letters of Vishaham's teacher and dear friend, Sir Madhava Rao.

From Trivandrum I was seen off, one evening, by Mr. Vieyra, the kindly Chief Secretary. My returning course now lay due north to Cochin, three nights' journey by cabin-boat, along the track by which I had entered Travancore. I need not repeat details. Under another moon, I had much the same lagoon experiences as three weeks before. This method of progression, by cabin-boat, is probably doomed, save for the stretch of 40 miles between Trivandrum and Quilon, which is along narrow canals, where steamboats cannot run. 'Forty miles from the railway, and forty years behind the times,' Trivandrum has been called. The only way is to link it up to some convenient station of the Quilon-Tinnevelly Railway. The cabin-boats are without the tolerable comfort even of a Kashmir doonga. They would be utterly impossible to live in.

I smile to think of the dream of renewing Kashmir experiences on these picturesque unknowable waters. The steamboats have been called more comfortable than the cabin-boats. I have my doubts, having seen a steamboat dragging along in the afternoon glare, hours late through having grounded on shoals. I would not for much have been without my six nights' experience of 'the oars of Ithaca.' Fourteen oars I counted, returning. I may say that, at least for December and January, mosquitoes are one of the empty bugbears of Malabar. I found practically no mosquitoes, even in the narrow canals; nor had once to submit to the indignity of sleeping within the sepulchral mosquito nets. The curse of petty animal life was in every respect greatly less than I had expected in such exuberant tropical regions.

On the way back, I spent four days at the glorious Quilon Residency, overlooking the salt Loch Katrine. The good Diwan Peshkar was unfortunately ill. Another Tehsildar, also a pleasant man, received me this time.

The vehicles of Quilon are fearsome things, and it is better to walk, except in the sun. Indeed, it is a point of superiority here, as compared to Trivandrum, that you can walk. One feels a distinct amelioration in the climate, even from the difference of two-thirds of a degree. This is not quite the brazen, sand-refracted heat of Trivandrum. It is barely possible to get through the day without the crumbling of all the faculties in the siesta of crushed repose. A foul plague of wind, the precursor of the hot season, persecuted us for the last two days. Neither at Quilon nor at Trivandrum did I see or hear of that infallible proof of a good Indian climate, namely, retired or unoccupied Europeans living there because they like the place, and wish to die there.

One of the days was very fully occupied in journeying across Travancore to meet the Diwan at Shenkota on the frontier, where he had been for some days on his return from the Christmas holidays in Madras, and in returning with him to Quilon. This was the journey which did not quite come off when I was in Quilon before. It rather suggests the Grecian days: 'When men might cross a kingdom in a day.' Travancore, as large as Wales, about one-third the size of all Greece, could never have been crossed twice in a day without the help of steam. The breadth of the State where the railway crosses it, in not quite its widest part, is about 60 miles. This distance is done in somewhat over four hours. The journey is through the same far-stretching Western Ghats, here in their lowest extension, wooded, green, and pleasant, but no longer first-rate, either for size or looks.

The trains do not run by night, though it is hard to see why they should not, since the line nowhere rises over 2000 feet. A train leaves Quilon at 6 a.m. If you take this, it is better to sleep aboard in the station. The first-class carriages are comfortable. Shenkota is 600 or 700 feet above the sea, and you feel the elevation instantly. Here you can possess your soul, here you can read without dizziness. This is Tamil country. The dark women in bright garments are unexpectedly comely, much better-looking than the men. The Tehsildar in charge here was pot of the grade of others I had met, and spoke hardly any English. A second-class Travellers' Bungalow, where the Diwan courteously called. But I must not begin speaking, at the fag-end of an article, about Diwan Bahadur P. Rajagopalachariar. Prime Minister of Travancore.

Chapter Thirteen - The Diwan of Travancore - Conclusion

IT is truly a remarkable group of Diwans which the three Southern States now possess. In each State, and elsewhere, I had heard claims that a particular Diwan was the very ablest of all. In Cochin, where Mr. Rajagopalachariar ruled for a quinquennium, until four or five years ago, I found his most convinced admirers. That is much, for there is every temptation to run down an ex-Diwan. These three strong men, between whom I am not going to institute comparisons, vary by an Indian generation in age. Mr. Madhava Rao is fifty-seven, Mr. Rajagopalachariar is forty-five, Mr. Banerji is thirty-six. Perhaps the middle one has made the best speed for his years. He has known, and will know, how to be strong within bounds.

His has been a victorious career. During a year of his youth, at the Madras Bar, Mr. Rajagopalachariar made a lot of money. He is still apt to wish, in moments of disillusionment, that he had never abandoned the Law. But he was caught up, nearly twenty years ago, into the Statutory Civil Service, the exact counterpart of which does not exist on the Bombay side. The members of this service do the work of Civilians, and get, not very equitably, two-thirds the pay. As a Collector, for example, a Statutory Civilian will get 1600 rupees. This is a point which naturally hurts the self-love of all Indians in a district. A good example was sot when the salaries of all members of the Madras High Court, European or Native, were equalised.

How shall I give, in a paragraph, some idea of half a dozen hours of close conversation with Mr. Rajagopalachariar? The southernmost Diwan knows Malabar as hardly any one, not born on the coast, can know it. His experience dates from eighteen or more years ago, when he was an Assistant Collector in British Malabar. It will be seen that he has governed steadily southwards. Travancore is in some respects the most difficult portion of Malabar to rule. The Diwan will not attempt it without the guidance and support of the experienced Maharaja, for whom he has a genuine admiration. I have expressed elsewhere his appreciation of some of the sterling qualities, the steadiness and the sense of continuity, of this sovereign.

I have never met a man of the Diwan's position who had less nonsense or fewer affectations. He would probably not shrink from the designation of 'a plain man.' He is all there, stripped for work, with immense driving power when once a channel is assured. His ideals, though he may not care for the adjective, seem Anglo-Saxon. On the railway journey down to Quilon there were deputations drawn up on several platforms, and specially at the terminus. I repeatedly saw the Diwan the centre of a group of which he was the poorest-dressed member.

On another day I rowed across from the Quilon Residency to an inferior building on the other side of Loch Katrine, the so-called Travalli Palace, where the Diwan was lodging. It was a comfortless palace, a palace of work. I told him that he gave his guests better accommodation than he gave himself. In Trivandrum he is said to occupy but a corner of his fine official palace, the Bhakti Vilasam. He is a widower, with five children, none of whom are with him in Travancore.

On that last day I found Mr. Rajagopalachariar, in connection with some recent official discovery, frankly denouncing 'the cursed tendency in Native States to go to sleep standing up.' That is what he will have to struggle with, the standing inertia of the East. It may prove too strong for him. Even climatically, it is bound to be more insidious in Travancore than anywhere else. It is little to say that there is nothing tonic about Travancore. The climate alone would make the land atonic, depressing, dissolving, not to say demoralising.

The Diwan has an unusual grasp of European history. His experience, already long, though he still seems a young man, has taught him a vital difference between Europeans and Indians. The educated native is undoubtedly the cleverer, the more intellectual, quicker 'in the uptake.' But it is all no good. It is so much ability in the air. The typical native lacks executive ability, constancy. The average Englishman has a rather thick head to drive an idea into. But once he grasps an order, he is admirably steady and faithful in carrying it out. He is an executive servant for his superiors to delight in. In the ideal distribution of posts in India, Mr. Rajagopalachariar feels that natives ought to occupy all posts up to 150 (£10) or 200, even 250, rupees a month — all merely subordinate ones. Englishmen, for one thing, can hardly live on such pay without corruption. In the middle grade, up to 750 (£50) or 1000 rupees, two-thirds of all posts should be filled by natives, and only one-third by Europeans. But in the highest grade, the directing grade, two-thirds of all posts should be filled by Europeans, and only one third by natives. That is, the real direction of affairs must remain European.

There is one exceptional department, the educational. This ought to remain under English control, regardless of the above proportions. The Diwan dates the beginning of disaffection from the time, about a generation ago, when we let the High Schools of the country pass out of our hands. There used to be a grade of Englishmen, content to draw only from 300 (£20) to 600 rupees a month as Headmasters of High Schools. They lived in isolation from most other Europeans, and in the happiest touch with native life. Their influence, and often that of their wives, upon the rising generation, was incalculable. The Diwan has the most grateful recollection of such a pair in his own early life. Since the English have been accepted as the rulers of India, they must, above all things, retain the direction of thought and education.

From Quilon I returned in the cabin-boat, a night's journey of 40 miles, to the lonely wayside bungalow at Karumadi, almost surrounded by water. Here, as before, an official was waiting to receive me, and a good table was set before me in the wilderness throughout a long day. By the Diwan's orders I was taken, in the twilight, to see' some houses of quite poor Nairs. Their standard of comfort and neatness is, as already noted, not that of Cochin, yet above that of most parts of India.

My kind conductors had both times arranged that I should pass in the night by Alleppey, where the cholera was bad. This is a town of commercial importance, not wholly incommensurate with that of its namesake on the Syrian coast, Travancore broadens steadily as you proceed northward. Of all this inland territory I had seen nothing save for the run across by railway. Prom Alleppey one proceeds naturally eastward to Kottayam, a great centre of the Syrian Christians, and also of missionary work.

It was a real loss to miss the life on the eastern mountains, where it is sometimes cool. There, if anywhere, may be found a European living in Travancore from pure choice, 'for climate and the affections.' There, also, are said to be the only feverish parts of the country. I had heard much, in conversation, of Peormadc, and of the great waterworks at Pcriar. The importance of all this in the life of the State should not bo lost sight of.

The last night's journey was a long one, about 50 miles, from Karumadi to Ernakulam. There were to be four relays; and I realised how impossible it was to know anything of the sixty-four human beings who were engaged in transporting me through the night. They sang, wildly, though not disturbingly. They dislike this boatwork, as in Kashmir; and the Government has to exercise a gentle compulsion, as well as to pay them well. There was much efficiency in the way in which the relays of rowers were silently changed.

There is little real blackness in Malabar; but it would be found among these semi-aquatic lagoon dwellers, if anywhere. Mr. A. P. Smith asserts that a very black girl is here considered more desirable than a more or less brown one, having often better features. The fact, which cannot hold for the whole of Travancore, must be an ethnological curiosity.

My last set of rowers lost the 10 a.m. train. I had thus an unexpected delay with friends old and new in Ernakulam. But first I wired to H.H. the Maharaja of Travancore my grateful thanks 'for twenty days of regal hospitality.'

The climate of Ernakulam presents a very sensible amelioration as compared with that of Trivandrum. There are 130 miles between; and every few miles make a difference. Mosquito nets arc not indispensable. In comparison with Trivandrum, one no longer feels like a worm here. I am encouraged to hope that another 130 miles up the Malabar coast may give a human climate to live in. The Europeans of Ernakulam and Cochin are to be commended for the high moral standard which they maintain, despite many temptations to the contrary.

After surrendering the hospitality of the State, I re-entered Travancore territory, which here cuts in at the back of Cochin, as the guest of a friend for a couple of days. A lonely Forest Bungalow, in teak plantations on the bank of the great Periar River — naturally the idea fascinated me. On starting for

Malabar, I had asked what was the characteristic product of that land, in order that I might bring back some. The answer was teak, with requests for cither some thousand cubic feet, or a few tons. Another product as genuine was ivory, of which alone I brought back any. But elephants were combined with teak in my friend's charge.

A clerk from the Forest Bungalow had been awaiting me in Ernakulam for several days. The bungalow is only about 20 miles from Ernakulam — but what miles! The dozen miles or so by rail, to a wayside station, are all right. But then came half a dozen miles in that true invention of the Devil, the bullock-cart. There followed four miles in a covered canoe, being rowed and pulled up the one big river of Travancore, the Periar. Even at this season, in January, it is still a noble stream, with banks almost brimming, above which rise young teakwoods. Any journey on the river is pleasant, even against the stream, or with occasional rapids to shoot. I, who had hitherto despised the 'wollam' or canoe as a cheap means of lagoon navigation, can now believe that it may be no more uncomfortable than the cabin-boat.

A large bungalow, above the broad stream. On the other side, a bathing house, whence noble bathing is to be had. A little up river, the shy Nair women may be seen disporting themselves in the water. My friend, a keen forester and botanist, able to name every shrub that grows. A typical athletic Englishman in physique and in tastes, delighting in long woodland excursions, regardless of the sun, which make one as hard as nails. Also a literary man, who ought someday to produce a book on the life of 'The Forest Officer,' written with a good deal more intimate knowledge than Mrs. Penny's amiable effort of that name.

This is the elephant country. An elephant, pitted a day or two before, was the objective of an expedition which filled most of our one whole day together. I had not imagined that it was possible, 10 degrees from the equator, to affront the sun with such impunity, and possibly even benefit. But, as I remember Sir William Hunter saying at Oxford:

'The Indian sun is a bad fellow; you mustn't take liberties with him!'

Yet I was none the worse, once in a way, for six miles upriver, several miles through jungle, then half a mile of sink, dive, wade, or swim, up the half-dried bed of a stream. My friend marched right ahead through whatever element offered, while I, and a ranger who was not strong, were carried when necessary. The elephant in the pit, at the end, was an interesting sight, though it was young, and without any vicious look in the small eyes. Elephants past the age of forty are released when caught, as being no longer capable of training. Our return was down a mile or two of half-dried channel. My friend rode stately on the bare neck of an elephant, where my own efforts to sit had been picturesque and vain.

So good-bye to 'our wild and sweet South-West.' Wild the people of Malabar certainly are, in the sense of the French 'farouche' — wildly shy. Of all peoples not mere sour fanatics, like some Northern Moslems, these must be the hardest to get acquainted with. They flow away from you, as I have elsewhere said, like quicksilver. Even when in seemingly frank contact with you, I am warned that they do not communicate their real selves. Here, again, the elusiveness is due to the abominable caste feeling. Stri-Malabar, forsooth! In few Hindu lands can it be more difficult even to speak to a woman. But the shyness is also local. To a singular degree, a European settled in Malabar comes to be accepted by the people. The moral tone of British India is somehow healthier. The peculiar status of Europeans in Native States, their conspicuousness, and the cognisance, not always devoid of espionage, which the Resident exercises over them, may be necessary, but are (as sometimes illustrated in Kashmir) emphatically not nice.

Some of the best men I met have been unmentioned. What could I have done without my hosts in Travancore? I would also have been badly off without Bob Antony, from whom I parted with real regret and respect. The rest is silence. But the last name must be that of one without whom these chapters would not have been possible. It is that of a great gentleman, by nature as by position. It is that of the Diwan of Mysore, whose two years in Travancore are there remembered as a little Golden Age — Mr. V. P. Madhava Rao, C.I.E.

Chapter Fourteen - The Administration of Mysore
(On the way to Malabar)

I HAVE been asked to give my impressions of the Administrations of Mysore, Cochin, and Travancore. For long I did not know how I could adequately respond to such a request. Obviously I cannot speak about these States with the same fulness of knowledge as about Kashmir. With regard to the great realm of Mysore, which is the second State in India (the area of Scotland, with more than the nominal population), but through which I was merely passing, I especially felt my inadequacy to say anything with authority. It was a case (as it so constantly is with us in this complex and varied world of India) of Keats's 'Standing aloof in giant ignorance.'

A week ago my ignorance about Mysore was extreme, if not engaging, candid and complete. I could not even have told what was the prevailing language of the country. Anything I may now tell will therefore be exposed to the reproach of being new knowledge. However, some special agencies have been at work to provide that I should see things correctly, and in the right focus. I blush to think that similar facilities were lately being provided for Mr. Keir Hardie.

But for a week past I have done nothing if not watch the Administration of Mysore from pretty near the centre. The chief fountain of my knowledge, as of the courtesies extended to me, has been the well-known Diwan, whom, by way of compliment, there is no need to name. It would be an impertinence to call such a man 'enlightened'; but I am not here writing a character sketch of him. In addition to the Diwan, I have conversed closely, for hours each, with some half-score officers of the State. I have been whirled over the country-side in motors, and have been personally conducted through villages. Let me at least tell a part of what I have seen and heard for the benefit of those who may know even less.

I shall quote freely from things that have been said to me. Unless indicated as such, these opinions must not be taken as being personally those of the Diwan.

Where shall I begin? The following are some of the predominant impressions left: Efficiency and simplicity of administration; up-to-date enlightenment in all public matters, as contrasted with some social ones; the amazingly high economic standard of a rather uninteresting people. One striking note of the place is expressed in the name of a leading Bangalore Club: the Cosmopolitan. This cosmopolitanism is considered by some to be overdone. I have counted four Faiths in the small group of most interesting men who are apt to gather around the Diwan on his verandah of a morning. It is, as one of the frequenters of the gathering says, 'a nice mixture.' The Diwan has said; 'I am colour-blind about religious differences.' He, or the State, is equally colour-blind about the place of origin of a good public servant. I wanted to carry off bodily, for examination, a charming and a specially busy man, the first Syrian Christian I had ever seen, who happens to be the Under-Secretary of State.

The Maratha colony at Tanjore has long been a nursery for Indian administrators, racially, for one thing, obviously superior to the Mysore people. The Mahomedans, if an outsider may judge, are less well regarded than are most. The State Service includes Englishmen, Eurasians, Parsis, Bengalis, Madrasis, Travancoreans, Mysoreans. That is the rub, that the people of Mysore should form only a fraction in their own Service. I have found three Mysoreans among the half-score officers I have seen most of. Even these are apt not to be fully indigenous. It is not strange that there are here two factions, the 'Mysoreans' and the 'foreigners.' I have heard it said that Mysore could not get along without the English over-rule, for that alone prevents the two parties from flying at each other's throats. That may be too strongly expressed.

Just as in Travancore, there is here much jealousy about the Diwan being so often brought from abroad. Yet the Diwanship preceding, which was that of a Mysorean, is stated not to have been a success. This is obviously a question upon which a stranger cannot form an opinion. But, in a large sense, Mysore seems to have many of the more admirable features of a democracy. It is government for the people, if not altogether by the people. The last element is not neglected.

I had vaguely supposed the Representative Assembly to be a sort of toy. Not at all. It has been in successful running since the Rendition, more than a quarter of a century ago. The Diwan believes it to be not merely a safety-valve, but a real and a largo factor in the well-being of the country. Though it sits for but one week in the year (October), its opinions, freely expressed, are seriously regarded. It helps keep the people happy and contented. They not only feel that they have a hand in conducting their own affairs, but they really have it. The Diwan would like to see the same factor at work in British territory.

Another democratic feature in Mysore is the fact that socially it is almost a dead level. There are few distinctions of rank save those due to officialdom — which, of course, is a state of things always liable to degenerate into a bureaucracy. The single great hereditary noble in the land is the late Diwan (Sir Krishna Murti). He, by the way, is remembered, by Europeans and others, for the quality of a nobleman, personal geniality. Nowhere is so much money spent as in Mysore upon local purposes — which is about the Radical ideal at Home. In few Indian lands is there so much money to spend, owing to the Kolar Gold Field, and to other causes. The ideal seems to be genuinely the greatest happiness of the greatest number.

Mysore is evidently, when one stops to think of it, the Canarese kingdom, the Canarese nation, flung between the Marathas and the Tamils. It was long a sort of buffer State; and a buffer State is seldom one of strong personality. But the Canarese people are now having their revenge over their neighbours. I have nowhere seen such a level of popular prosperity and cleanliness in India or in Kashmir. I could write an article on the two towns, a large village and a Taluka centre, through which I was somewhat minutely taken. It was a revelation. Such spotless cleanliness of streets, courtyards, and houses; such decent, human habitations, in which one could live oneself without the certainty of snuffing out.

Such excellent, neat clothing, even for children of an age who would everywhere else go naked. And the average income per house, apparently, six or eight rupees (about half a pound) — or less. I suspect that the living of the people is of less striking excellence than their housing and their clothing; but into this question of food I cannot go. It is the common people who everywhere count, economically. And all the things which a quite poor man needs seem here to be of the cheapest. That is surely a democratic consummation. Everywhere I noticed little signs of the civilising superfluous — not only the bare needful, but something over.

I asked how many officers there were drawing Rs. 600 (£33 odd) a month or over. The answer was: 'Three hundred.' The Mysore Provincial Service, unlike that in British India, is recruited by competitive examination. I have known two (confessedly picked men) out of the 68 Amildars of the State. About 10 per cent of them are admitted to be bad. But they get into trouble, for the Diwar is death on corruption.

Everywhere I was told that the beginnings of the prosperity I saw were the work of Englishmen. But the good work is being carried on by Indians; and, I am told, better than Englishmen could do it now. Indians can watch

65

their subordinates better; they are simpler, cheaper, more in touch with the people. The conclusion, which the Diwan endorses, is that Englishmen are best fitted to initiate, but Indians to carry on, such work.

'There is no intrigue in Mysore,' the Diwan once said proudly. Others have told me there is some intrigue here, but less than in any other Native State. A keen officer told me that, after a little, Mysore might even equal the standard of Baroda, where there is such an admirable and leonine ruler, more able than any of his own Ministers. The present Diwan thinks that the standard is already higher here, since it does not depend upon any one man. He believes the prosperity and efficiency in Mysore to be greater than in any other territory, British or Native. And he dates this special rush of progress from the Rendition, in 1881. That is humiliating for us, who like to pat ourselves on the back for that act. But to think that the Mysore people began to be truly happy from the day we let them go! There are depths of Home Rule sentiment in the Diwan, and in my other friends here, which I have not dared or cared to explore. I do not know what conclusions to draw. Mysore is the right kind of *Swadeshi*. It is also *Swaraj* (Self-Rule).

Chapter Fifteen - The Administration of Cochin
(a fragment)

I HAVE long noted the wholly disproportionate amount of attention which Kashmir has always attracted throughout the centuries. The modern Kashmir State is, to be sure, one of the most considerable in India; but it is the Valley, of less than 2000 square miles, which is so famous. In a more local way the tiny State of Cochin has attracted an attention almost as disproportionate. It is about one-thousandth part of the area of what used to be the Indian Empire, before Burma and Baluchistan were added on either side. By population, of course, Cochin is more nearly one three-hundredth part. Its area, again, is roughly one-hundredth part that of the Madras Presidency. It is necessary to remember every fraction of it — 1361 ½ square miles. It is one-quarter the size of many a British District.

When the Raja is stated to know every detail of its administration one is tempted to answer flippantly that such knowledge need not be extensive. You could almost fling your shoe, in Scripture phrase, over parts of the State. It recalls, what with the way Travancore cuts into it at the back. Max Müller's jest about how you could not throw a stone, in some of the German States of his youth, without danger of its falling across the frontier.

But Cochin (which is still apt to be confused, at home, with Cochin-China) is important and interesting wholly out of proportion to its size. Nowhere, probably, is there so small a territory so richly diversified both in its natural features and in its inhabitants. A third part of the State consists of rich forests, containing unequalled teak and rosewood. Here are a few woodland tribes, some of them living on platforms in tree tops: elephants are the enemy. This leaves a density of some 1000 per square mile for the remainder of the State. The mere quarter part of the population who are Christian boast between them at least half a dozen Prelates of sorts. Bishops and Archbishops. The Hindus are among the most exclusive, and at the same time most curiously tolerant, in the world. The last trait is illustrated by the fact of their now having a Brahmo Diwan.

I have been given a book about Cochin, which would make several delightful days of reading, the first volume of the 'Census Report,' by Mr. Sankara Menon. I have been offered other material, and interesting too, which might have been digested by 'the giant race before the Flood.' Cochin, when not grossly mismanaged, naturally hums with prosperity. Much of the great interest which it excites is inevitable and permanent.

All this, however, has been intensified, since the beginning of the year now ending, by the appointment of Mr. Albion R. Banerji as Diwan. Both as a member of the Indian Civil Service, and personally, he offers some guarantees never before equalled by an Indian Diwan. His work is constantly being discussed in the Press of Southern India. But few can realise the bulk which these discussions have already reached. Cuttings from some ten Indian and Anglo-Indian newspapers, on the subject of Cochin, within this year, fill two large scrap-books. They would, together, make a good-sized volume, and one of considerable interest. They chiefly concern the reforms restlessly initiated or suggested. About the details of these, even the fools who write letters to the Editor know more than I can possibly hope to, though I have been granted every facility and aid, though I have met more Heads of Departments than I can count.

Mr. Banerji is constantly compared to the expert engineer, employed to set machinery right by tightening it up here, throwing out a rejected screw there. Naturally, the rejected screws hate him! But it is interesting to have him testify to the reasonableness of the Native Press in its comments and demands, as representing a public really worthy of respect. His principle seems to be efficiency, although on a somewhat small scale. 'In small measures, men may perfect be.' After all, the income of Cochin, Rs. 35 lakhs (£233,310), is more than one-third that of great Kashmir. Mr. Banerji evidently has no patience with the dangerous tendency often expressed in the east by *Festina lente*. There are in Cochin but five Tehsildars (lately seven), as compared with 31 in Travancore, and 68 in Mysore. There is but one Diwan Peshkar (lately two), as compared with four in Travancore. Things are done more economically here. Of officers drawing Rs. 500 or more per month, of whom there are 300 in Mysore, Cochin has barely a dozen.

After a week here employed in nothing but learning, I feel myself more utterly ignorant, more incompetent to give an opinion, than after a similar or longer period in Mysore. The people seem at least equally prosperous with those in Mysore. They are much more strange, also much more dainty. There is something delicate and graceful in the very sight of the little girls walking about with their reed umbrellas. Here is a civilisation which, though we cannot understand it, evidently deserves respect. For such a people, already thriving and intelligent, Mr. Banerji is doing his best, which is much. How does his position compare with that of a Collector? There is greatly more circumstance, responsibility, power of initiative, opportunity, and inspiration. He is fortunate above all in his youth. He may be on the verge of a truly great career.

* * * * *

Chapter Sixteen - The Administration of Travancore

A COUNTRY about as large as Wales, and at least as variegated. The very shape is not unlike that of the Principality. There is a similar combination of mountains and of sea. The population of Travancore is not only greater than that of Wales, at present, but vastly greater than that of historic Wales, which probably never exceeded a hundred thousand.

In Trivandrum intellect is said to be a drug on the market, and to go begging. A narrow, an unpractical, a merely literary talent it has been called; yet it is much. A complicated country, with a long and thrilling history, of which practically no Englishman knows anything. How a cultured Travancorean's face will light up at the mention of the ancient Kingdom of Shera, which is the Tamil for Kerala!

It is still the home of a social system, the matriarchal, which is singularly elusive and hard to understand, which exists nowhere else among a civilised people. That the Malabar people are civilised there is no manner of room for doubt. This is what makes them unique — the grafting of Brahmanical institutions upon a matriarchal system of society. It also seems to make them peculiarly elusive, hard to understand. They are said to be not exactly shy. But they flow away from the stranger like quicksilver.

A country of 3,000,000 people, of a prosperity which is indicated by its revenue of Rs. 100 lakhs (£666,666). A country never conquered, it is to be noted, by the British. It is a point of pride for Travancore that to this day any disputed question must be settled by a reference to Treaty stipulations. It is only owing to quite peculiar local circumstances that a State of this size and importance depends upon Madras, and not upon the Government of India. There is no other instance of a Presidency controlling a State of this class. The circumstances which brought this about were largely geographical, 'This last corner' — as I have heard Travancore aptly defined. The Madras Presidency would now feel lost without this noble southmost State. It offers to Madras Civilians a culminating post which, though not the highest, must be far more interesting and romantic than some posts which outgrade it.

But even greater is the debt of Travancore to Madras. I have heard much lately of the exceptionally wise spirit of moderation which actuates the Madras Government. In the Madras Presidency (sometimes called, in India, the Benighted Presidency), which almost ought to be called the enlightened, there seems to be a happy touch between the people and the administrators. I can only judge from the outside. But the vicious spirit of faction seems to be as remote as is any danger of famine. When there are political contests, by a tacit and highly honourable convention, which does not exist at present in all parts of India, women are regarded as being outside party. It has been a great relief, during the last six weeks, to find myself beyond even the ignoble echoes of any sedition.

In vain I inquire how Madras produces such good administrators, since few of them have gone there originally from choice. Madras seems to shape these men to its purposes despite themselves. There is something telling in the inherited spirit of the administration, from a period far antedating Monro. A point which would make a good leader, but which I can only indicate here, is this: the importance of having the Madras tradition of breadth and tolerance more largely represented at the India House; for Governments are not so wise in all parts of India. The Madras people are, to be sure, especially easy to govern; yet they might be mishandled. All this noble Madras tradition Malabar has had the reflected benefit of during a century. At this moment, two Madras Civilians administer the two Malabar States.

Still, what can a stranger say of profit about the Travancore Administration? I have at least been enabled to see things from as nearly as possible the centre. During several weeks I have journeyed up and down Travancore, and also across it by railway, at the expense of the State. I have met the Maharaja, the little Ranis, the venerable Kerala Varma, C.S.I., the Diwan, the Chief Secretary, and various Heads of Departments. I have known two out of the four Diwan Peshkars, and five out of the thirty-one Tehsildars.

Now what shall I say of the last, the Tehsildars? I have known this grade of officer all the way southward from Kashmir — but nowhere more suave than in Travancore. These Tehsildars are generally B.A.'s, drawing from Rs. 125 to Rs. 200 a month. To me they appeared to be charming men — naturally, since they were largely engaged in caring for my wants. This they did with much efficiency. But the business of an Opposition is to oppose. The business of Revenue Officers is to collect revenue, and to dispose promptly of cases connected therewith. Now I am arrested by this sentence in the Diwan's Address to the Sri Mulam Popular Assembly in November: 'Work of Peshkars and Tehsildars: Government are unable to speak of the work of these officers with satisfaction.' What can I add?

It is notorious that alike in Mysore, Cochin, and Travancore, specially able Diwans have lately been called in after a period of muddlement. In Trivandrum, the Chief Secretary, Mr. A. J. Vieyra, keeps things running smoothly during any temporary absence of the Diwan. At the Public Offices I was pleased to see a son-in-law of the late very able Maharaja, with the right to be called Raja himself, working away at Rs. 400 a month as Under-Secretary for Education. This is unlike the state of things in Cochin, where the very numerous Princes (40 of them!) are being trained to earn their living abroad.

Of each of the three southern Diwans I have heard it claimed that he is the very ablest of the three. I can at least understand this claim for Mr. Rajagopalachariar after having talked closely with him. No Diwan, surely, can have less nonsense about him, less affectation, less waste of force. He suggests an athlete concentrated for work; and yet he will go carefully, avoiding upsetting things. He has obviously hardly begun his work as yet. The official literary man of the State, and a clever one, is Mr. Nagam Aiya, author of the 'State Manual.' He has served as Acting Diwan not less than five times; and had claims to the substantive appointment, had it not been considered necessary to bring in once more, as so often before, a man from outside the State. The present Diwan has known the Malabar Coast, off and on, for eighteen years, both in British Malabar and as Diwan of Cochin.

I also hear Mr. Madhava Rao everywhere spoken of as a noble gentleman, large-hearted and large-minded, whose two years here were a little Golden Age for Travancore. I get glimpses of parties that pull pretty violently — Nairs against Brahmans, and native Travancoreans against so-called foreigners. The Maratha Brahmans from Tanjore, known as Raos, have an amazing predominance in politics, with some natural gift for administration; and next to them come the Tamil Brahmans. The elusive quality of the Malabar people proper seems to hold, even in politics. They slip away from the best posts, though much against their will!

Of officers drawing Rs. 500 or more per month there are in Mysore 300, and in Cochin hardly a dozen. In Travancore there are 30. A Native State is dreadfully apt to change its whole policy with each Diwan that comes. This tendency to oscillation is naturally most marked in the smallest States, which are most easily set in motion. Mr. Rajagopalachariar sees a safeguard against this tendency in Travancore in the equable character of the Maharaja's mind. His Highness is said to have a genius for continuity of policy. If once convinced of the excellence of a given measure, he can hold steadily to it through successive Diwanships. He has had but six Diwans, not counting the present one, in twenty-two years.

It is interesting to hear the Diwan's warm praises of the work done, in one week per year, by the still new Popular Assembly. The entire machinery of State seems to stand still for a week, while it is overhauled from top to bottom. Travancore takes splendidly to this democratic institution. Of the members the Diwan says: 'They are all clever.' That is a tremendous thing to say of 100 men. They are also just, and eminently practical.

www.ingramcontent.com/pod-product-compliance
Lightning Source LLC
Chambersburg PA
CBHW020557130626
46552CB00007B/2929